Romance

AND THE EROTICS OF PROPERTY

Mass-Market Fiction for Women

Jan Cohn

Duke University Press 1988

Durham and London

© 1988 Duke University Press
All rights reserved
Printed in the United States of America
on acid-free paper ∞

Library of Congress Cataloging-in-Publication Data
Cohn, Jan, 1933–
Romance and the erotics of property/Jan Cohn.
Bibliography: p.
Includes index.
ISBN 0-8223-0799-5
1. Love stories, American—History and criticism.   2. American
fiction—20th century—History and criticism.   3. Popular
literature—United States—History and criticism.   4. Women—United
States—Books and reading.   5. Property in literature.   I. Title.
PS374.L6C6   1988
813'.085'09—dc19   87-27401

Designed by Anne Keyl

*For
my mother
and
my daughter*

CONTENTS

ACKNOWLEDGMENTS

vii

INTRODUCTION

I

1

SEX, LOVE, AND MARRIAGE

13

2

THE ROMANCE HERO

39

3

THE VICTORIAN POPULAR ROMANCE

63

4

WOMEN'S WORK

93

5

THE EROTICS OF PROPERTY

125

6

ROMANCE AND SEXUAL POLITICS

151

INDEX

179

ACKNOWLEDGMENTS

My study of romance has been guided through a series of metamorphoses by friends and former colleagues in the English Department at George Mason University. Devon Hodges, Deborah Kaplan, Eileen Sypher, and Peter Brunette all read the manuscript at different stages and all provided sensitive and shrewd critiques. I am grateful for their help and indebted as well to a number of other former colleagues in the department who sustained the special intellectual climate that helped foster this work. As for the personal climate, both intellectual and emotional, my loving indebtedness, as always, to Bill.

INTRODUCTION

The link between reader and writer
forged by every popular book is a mystic one.
The writer may not know all he has said;
the reader all he has heard;
yet they understand each other perfectly.

—Helen Papashvily, *All the Happy Endings*

This book offers a reading of romance. "Romance," to be sure, is a deeply ambiguous term, and one I shall consider in several ways; initially, however, I wish to address it in the specific sense of contemporary *popular romance*, the type of mass fiction created and marketed for women and exemplified by Harlequin novels, which tells the story of how a modern young woman succeeds in marrying a handsome, desirable, and wealthy man. Put more simply, it tells the story of how the heroine simply *succeeds*, for in conventional, which is to say politically conservative, terms, her only possible success in our society comes in marrying happily and marrying well. Put more polemically, popular romance tells the story of how the heroine gains access to money—to power—in patriarchal society. In thousands of books read by millions of romance readers, romance tells over and over a story about power deeply encoded within a story about love.

It is my thesis that power, not love, lies at the heart of the fictions of popular romance. In the fantasy gratification offered by contemporary popular romance are not only the secret sentimental and sensual delights of love but the forbidden pleasures of revenge and appropriation. In heavily coded structures these stories redistribute not only the power relations that exist within marriage, within the patriarchal family, but through and beyond that threaten existing gender relations in the broadest areas of power in patriarchal society itself.

The fantasy provided by popular romance exists to redress the real social and economic conditions of women in the world of the present; but the strategies and codes through which romance constructs and communicates fantasy have their roots in history, in the development of bourgeois society. They find their sources and analogues in the fictions bourgeois society elicited in novels of courtship and marriage, for the social contradictions that inform such novels are buried deep in romance stories, charging them with subversive energy.

No classic novels of courtship and marriage have contributed more to the development of the romance formula than Jane Austen's *Pride and Prejudice* and Charlotte Brontë's *Jane Eyre*. The success with which each of these novels yokes the exigencies of real historical conditions to the fantasy of romance gratification has endowed them with a special life in the romance imagination. The conception of the hero in these novels, the ways in which power and property are initially distributed, and the means by which their eventual redistribution creates a new equilibrium of male-female power are all wrenched free of the historical situations in which they were created to assume a transhistorical vitality captured as formula and stereotype.

Essentially, the legacy of Austen and Brontë lies in the character of the hero each created; much of the history of romance is the story of the ascendancy of the dark and sullied hero, Rochester, over the more perfect Darcy. But this was no easy victory, and one can measure the dilemma the changing hero caused romance fiction by looking at the work of two popular and prolific late Victorian romance writers, May Agnes Fleming and Harriet Lewis. Their heroines contend with both types of hero, but Darcy is vitiated, without power or property, and Rochester is a villain, sexual, threatening, and entirely unredeemable.

Not until Margaret Mitchell's *Gone with the Wind* was the problem of the hero resolved, which provides the third principal source for contemporary romance. Here, Darcy reappears as Ashley Wilkes, but he must confront and at last fall to the superior power of his dark twin, Rhett Butler. Nor can Twelve Oaks, the anachronistic echo of Darcy's Pemberley, survive. Instead of the landed estate, risk capital becomes the source of money and power as Mitchell allows the realities of the bourgeois economic order, itself played out anachronistically through an historical romance of the Civil War, finally to construct the plausible and potent romance hero.

Throughout the history of the romance hero, his principal avowed relation to the heroine has been predicated on the reader's expectation of a successful resolution in love. Contemporary romance inherits this tradition, for "romance" in popular usage is synonymous with "love story" and both romance and the love it celebrates occupy a central place in the female imagination. This is, to be sure, the result of a profound cultural change, a major legacy of bourgeois society. Love was once suffered by *lovers*, by men entranced, enthralled, held in thrall by the eyes and mouths and hair of unobtainable mistresses. But men are now busy elsewhere, and they have left the field of love to women. Women have become the experts in love; it is tempting to call them "amateurs." As it turns out, though, women are considerably less futile as lovers than men. Love has an appropriate use and a necessary consummation in marriage. So, if love continues, in popular romance, to torment its victim, it is no vain enterprise; at least it pays off.

The rewards of love in popular romance, however, are not precisely marriage per se, although matrimony is always included as a benefit; the real reward is the acquisition of the hero. The hero, moreover, is well worth acquiring because he carries within him all the power and authority of the patriarchy. In the structures of contemporary romance there is no way for the heroine to acquire that power except by acquiring the hero. Thus, the love story in contemporary romance fiction can be seen as a trope for what would otherwise be a forbidden exercise in female self-realization and the will to power.

Like all popular formula fiction, romance exists to answer in fantasy needs that cannot be met in real life. But romance goes further; it answers desires that cannot be spoken, so powerfully would they subvert authority. Desire and authority are profoundly at issue in popular romance. Desire, however, must be heavily masked since, at the deepest level, what is desired is authority itself, the power and autonomy the social system denies women. In the surface story of romantic and sensual love, desire is diminished to the conventional and acceptable longing for love and marriage. Yet even that non-threatening desire must be disguised. The heroine of romance must seem to seek *nothing*, as if to confess to desire in any form were to confess to the deeper, the vengeful and aggressive, desires that are forbidden.

✳ Authority is challenged only at the deepest levels of romance; on the surface romance embraces and confirms conventional values. As each story finds its resolution in marriage, it piously reaffirms the status of the patriarchal family. Even more significantly, the heroine's matrimonial success celebrates the patriarchal order as a whole; it is within that order, for all its confining strictures, that she wins her victory. The formulaic resolution of romance serves "to moralize reality," in Hayden White's phrase;[1] the authority that seemed, in the person of the hero, to frustrate, demean, and even torment the heroine turns out to be the source, even the very terms, of rescue and safety.

Romance reading provides a complex set of gratifications for vast numbers of women in our society who, much as feminists may lament it, feel more secure than threatened under the conditions of patriarchy, which, if restrictive and damaging, are at least familiar. In responding to the conflicting demands of authority and desire in its mix of social aggression and social conservatism, romance, like other forms of mass fiction, creates structures in which the reader's identification with the heroine allows her to experience emotions otherwise negatively sanctioned, to play out tabooed roles in defiance of the social order. Even the act of reading—since these are "only stories"—serves as protection for the reader enjoying the vicarious experience of the forbidden.[2]

1. The relationship of narrative to authority has been addressed by Hayden White, who argues that authority, specifically in the form of a legal system, is a necessary precondition for narrative. According to White, narrativity depends on "the existence of a legal system against or on behalf of which the typical agents of a narrative account militate." Thus, narrative from its simplest to its most sophisticated forms has to do with "*authority*," for narrative arises from "the *conflict* between desire, on the one side, and the law, on the other." White is not, to be sure, concerned in his discussion of the development of historical narrativity with the question of popular formula fiction. Nevertheless, his concept of narrative born of the tension between desire and authority is a powerful one for romance stories, especially since White contends that the function of historical narrative and perhaps of fictional narrative as well is "to moralize reality, that is, to identify it with the social system that is the source of any morality that we can imagine" ("The Value of Narrativity in the Representation of Reality," *Critical Inquiry* 7 [Autumn 1980]: 17–18).

2. Janice Radway notes the ritual aspect of romance reading, seeing that these stories "resemble the myths of oral culture in the sense that they exist to relate a story already familiar to the people who choose to read them." Thus, Radway makes the point that romance novels serve as "the ritualistic repetition of a single, immutable cultural myth" (*Reading the Romance: Women, Patriarchy, and Popular Literature* [Chapel Hill: University of North Carolina Press, 1984], p. 198).

In some ways the entire problem of love and power seems to come down to the deep ambiguities in the multivalent word, "romance." Against the meaning of romance, of popular romance, as a love story, stands the whole privileged literary history of Romance. It is useful to think of the surface story, the love story, as romance of the lowercase, unprivileged sort, and the subtext as somehow related to the "real thing," to literary Romance. Northrop Frye has written that "popular romance, in whatever media it may come, is often an expression of a frivolous or silly social mythology,"[3] and while I would not call the mythology of love and marriage frivolous, I would certainly agree that, as a mythology, it fails to cut to the heart of the issue—the issue of power and gender relations. Power and gender relations, however, are clearly addressed in the subtext of romance fictions, where these matters are resolved, again in fantasy, in favor of the weaker gender; power is acquired by the powerless. Here perhaps, coded and cautious, is Romance, an outlaw world where the forbidden is allowed, a magical world where the impossible occurs.

In recent years both Northrop Frye and Fredric Jameson have insisted on a connection between romance and popular literature. Frye, who includes in the category of popular romance such forms as the detective novel and the Western, argues that reading these stories, not in the terms of the individual work but the "entire convention," can "tell us a good deal about the shape of stories as a whole, and that, in its turn, would begin to give us some glimpse of still larger verbal structures, eventually of the mythological universe itself." Jameson attributes to Frye the conception of "the popular or mass culture of our own time [as] syllables and broken fragments of some single immense story." For Jameson, however, the real point is the historical reemergence of romance: "It is in the context of the gradual reification of realism in late capitalism that romance once again comes to be felt as the place of narrative heterogeneity and of freedom from that reality principle to which a now oppressive realistic representation is the hostage." From that point of view, the

3. Northrop Frye, *The Secular Scripture: A Study of the Structure of Romance* (Cambridge: Harvard University Press, 1976), p. 167.

subtext of contemporary popular romance is indeed a form of privileged Romance, a place where freedom from the reality of existing gender relations allows the fantastic redistribution of power.[4]

The remarkable thing about popular romance is the way the surface story of love and the subtextual story of power are linked, or, more precisely, how the love story encodes the power story. In Harlequin romances, love is the expressed value, marriage the goal, and sex the arena of conflict in the surface story, but all three become the terms for encoding the subtextual story of power—specifically, economic power. The encoding of the struggle for power in the formulaic structures of sexuality, love, and marriage is far from arbitrary. Emerging bourgeois, patriarchal society reduced women's economic function to her role in the marriage market. Upward mobility, promised at least in theory to all sober and industrious men, was denied her in her exclusion from the marketplace. Marriage was her only real economic resource; and marriage to a man socially and economically her superior, her only real chance for upward mobility, her only recourse to power. But such a marriage, however desirable it might in fact have been, was publicly denigrated; romantic love insisted that marriage be based on emotional rather than economic considerations.[5]

Contemporary popular romance has inherited the history of love and marriage along with its thick masking and deep contradictions. Therefore, popular romance necessarily tells a woman's story, but the central interest of romance remains fixed on the hero, sign of the patriarchy, enemy and lover. Granted economic dominance in a marketplace economy and cast in the role of sexual predator, the romance hero enjoys power precisely where women are most powerless. Nor is it merely a question of two coexisting forms of male power; sexual and economic dominance are intimately linked, a

4. Frye, *The Secular Scripture*, p. 60; Fredric Jameson, *The Political Unconsciousness: Narrative as Socially Symbolic Act* (Ithaca, N.Y.: Cornell University Press, 1981), pp. 105, 104.

5. Jenni Calder points to the connection between sexual and economic weakness in women, arguing that "the vulnerability of women . . . stems not just from their feminine weakness, but from their lack of economic status" (*Women and Marriage in Victorian Fiction* [New York: Oxford University Press, 1976], p. 17). See also Lawrence Stone, *The Family, Sex and Marriage* (New York: Harper and Row, 1977).

kind of reciprocal metaphoric relationship existing between them. Against this Janus-faced enemy the only weapon is love and the only victory, marriage. The fantasy gratification afforded by popular romance turns on these elements. In the fantasy constructed by the subtext, love and marriage become means for appropriating the power and dominance neither the real world nor even the conventional surface plot will allow. In the surface plot, conversely, love and marriage are taken at their conventional value, as rewards for good behavior, the bestowal of fabulous happiness in return for surrender to convention. The heroine must accept the role assigned her in patriarchal society, but in romance the cage of convention is richly gilded.

In the marriage of hero and heroine, romance fiction reaffirms its loyalty to convention and, at the same time, to the real, in the form of existing social conditions. This realistic view of women's roles, sugarcoated though it may be, is itself an echo of collective wisdom, a way of saying to readers, "Let's not kid ourselves; this is how it is for women." A mimetic quality, moreover, is an essential aspect of popular romance throughout the narrative.[6] Stories are carefully, if sketchily set to create a feeling of verisimilitude, for the intrusion of fantasy in the narrative elements would seriously jeopardize the strategies through which romance functions. The heroine of contemporary romance, at once unique and endlessly replicable, is significant for romance readers precisely because her world is "real," is ordinary, and the fantastic happy endings of romance have their power in direct relation to the apparent everyday quality of the heroine's life before she meets the hero, before romance—in two senses of the word—enters her life.

My reading of contemporary romance, therefore, is restricted to the particular subgenre that most carefully establishes a real-world setting, the better to enable the story to exploit the initial dichotomy between, and eventual fusion of, real life and romance. Harlequin romances and their imitators have this characteristic if for no other reason than their contemporary settings. Without recourse to a dis-

6. For a full discussion of the mix of mimetic and mythic narration in romance, see Radway, *Reading the Romance*, pp. 186–208.

9

tant historical period or to Gothic devices, these romances place their heroines in real places, whether New York or London or Boise, Idaho, and they establish their heroines in real situations, find them work to do during the time when, in the long tradition of the virtuous heroine, they are specifically engaged in *not* looking for husbands. Moreover, these romances must, by the very fact of their contemporaneity, be at least minimally responsive to social change, coping tentatively with new attitudes toward "liberation," both sexual and economic.

Though contemporary popular romance is formula fiction, a ritualized retelling of a fantasy victory over real social conditions, it is far from impervious to social change. The fact that the emergence of the women's movement in the late 1960s marks the beginning of the meteoric rise in popularity of Harlequin romances strongly suggests that these fictions serve to negotiate for their readers the dilemmas of social change. For many women, feminism exacerbated the contradictions in gender roles by threatening to undermine traditional rules for female behavior and the rewards anticipated for following those rules. Convention still dictated that economic survival depended on marriage, and for that reason women continued to value conservative feminine characteristics of modesty, passivity, and subordination. But the women's movement promised new independence—and specifically new economic independence—to women. Paradoxically, the promise of feminism carried a considerable threat, undercutting traditional gender relations, particularly in regard to courtship, and thereby putting women in jeopardy of failing in the marriage market.

The Harlequin romance, for all its banality, manages to negotiate this mine field with remarkable acuity, *adopting* to some extent the new models of female behavior for the heroine, *adapting* these models to an intricate system of valuation and devaluation, and continuing to reward the heroine with both marriage and, most significantly, male property.

Having constructed a formula that negotiates the heroine's success in achieving romantic love and simultaneously encodes her success in appropriating male property, the contemporary romance also manages to trim and adjust aspects of the stories it tells so as to maintain a degree of up-to-dateness. In some recent romances the heroine enjoys more professional and sexual freedom, reflecting current social changes in women's roles. Still, the formula remains constant as does the ideology romance espouses, and it is the formula that is at issue here.

This book, then, examines the way in which popular romance provides its "solutions." In it I have chosen to look at romance through a number of different lenses, sociological and historical and theoretical, but always return to contemporary romance itself, each time asking new and deeper questions about its formula and its coded messages. Chapter 1 explores the dynamic relationship among sex, love, and marriage, the key terms of the surface story of romance, developing at the same time a theory of romance as a form of Quest Romance for women. Chapter 2 turns to the romance hero, the sign of the patriarchy and at once the object of the heroine's quest and its antagonist. In studying the development of the contemporary romance hero, this chapter explores his roots in the inversion of hero and villain accomplished by Charlotte Brontë in the figures of Mr. Rochester and St. John Rivers. Chapter 3 looks at the sensational romances of two popular Victorian writers, Harriet Lewis and May Agnes Fleming, in whose stories we find the hero atomized into his several components in the figure of hero, villain, and surrogate father; against these separate figures of patriarchal power, the Victorian heroine plays out the violent themes of revenge and appropriation.

Chapter 4 turns to the question of work. Both Victorian and contemporary heroines enter the marketplace, Victorian heroines taking a first symbolic step toward autonomy and independence and contemporary heroines engaging in some activity that defends them against betraying their search for a husband. Work, however, is never the route to success and security for heroines in patriarchal society. Success and security rest in property, as chapter 5 argues, tracing the economics of romance fiction. In his economic glamour, the romance hero has his source in Jane Austen's Darcy, aristocrat and property owner. Anachronistically, economic power remained a function of inherited property in romance until Margaret Mitchell created her own reversal of hero and villain in Ashley Wilkes and

Rhett Butler, thereby providing romance fiction with a model for the hero who achieves power in the bourgeois marketplace. Chapter 6 looks at romance as the initiation of the heroine conducted under the mentorship of the glamorous and powerful hero. The heroine must *earn* her right to the mentor-hero, the reward for the successful accomplishment of her initiation. Chapter 6 addresses the problem of the price exacted from the heroine as the cost of her triumph and, concomitantly, the larger problem of the sexual politics of popular romance.

Popular romance, whatever its sexual politics, exists to provide, in Fredric Jameson's terms, "imaginary or formal 'solutions' to unresolvable social contradictions."[7] The social contradictions inherent in women's situation in patriarchal society are precisely what romance addresses, and because those contradictions remain unresolvable, it provides through fantasy gratification the only "solutions" it can imagine. "History," as Jameson says, "is what hurts."[7]

7. Jameson, *Political Unconsciousness*, pp. 79, 102.

1

SEX, LOVE, AND MARRIAGE

Men's novels are about how to get power.
Killing and so on, or winning, and so on.
So are women's novels, though the method is different.
In men's novels, getting the woman or women
goes along with getting the power. It's a perk
not a means. In women's novels you get the power
by getting the man. The man is the power. But sex won't do,
he has to love you. What do you think that kneeling's about,
down among the crinolines, on the Persian carpet?
Or at least say it. When all else is lacking,
verbalization can be enough. *Love*.
There, you can stand up now, it didn't kill you.
Did it?

Margaret Atwood, "Women's Novels"

$\mathcal{H}$arlequin understands how you feel about love."[1] In their advertisements for contemporary popular romances, publishers claim love as their subject and love as the common ground shared with each reader. These fictions hold out and fulfill the promise of love, offering the reader the chance to experience love herself—if only vicariously and in fantasy. Romance and love become nearly synonymous terms, each implying the other. As John Cawelti points out in *Adventure, Mystery, and Romance*, "The moral fantasy of the romance is that of love triumphant and permanent, overcoming all obstacles and difficulties."[2] But the spectacular success achieved by Harlequin and other romance publishers raises serious critical questions about the fantasy content of these stories and about their moral, which is to say political, credentials.

The romance industry may promise love, but many critics see

1. This particular advertisement appears on the back covers of Yvonne Whittal, *Seasons of Shadows* (New York: Harlequin Books, 1981). Harlequin romances explicitly advertise love, and scattered evidence from romance readers and writers supports the idea that love and not sex is what romances are all about. A few years ago, the *New York Times*, reporting on a party thrown by Harlequin vice president, Fred Kerner, for loyal New Jersey fans, explained that these stories have "no explicit sex. Which seems to be what Harlequin readers want." Two readers commented in support of that contention: "We have good imaginations," said one; and the other added, "We don't want the violence" (*New York Times*, 27 September 1980). In the first issue of *Romantic Times* in 1981, Barbara Michaels, who writes gothics under the name of Elizabeth Peters, writes to defend herself and her genre from the taint of pornography brought by "recent entries" into the field, "variously referred to as bodice rippers and soft porno Gothics." She acknowledges the sexual revolution and has no objection to the new morality, but points out that "heroines who are ravished every thirty pages represent [an] example of this not-so-suppressed antagonism toward women." Moreover, to have the hero's lust turn at the end "to true love . . . only makes matters worse. The message seems to be, rape a girl often enough, boys, and she'll grovel at your feet." This, asserts Michaels, is "not my idea of romance" (*Romantic Times* [July–August 1981]: 20).

For the most thorough investigation of romance readers and their responses to romance fiction, see Janice Radway, *Reading the Romance: Women, Patriarchy, and Popular Literature* (Chapel Hill: University of North Carolina Press, 1984).

2. John G. Cawelti, *Adventure, Mystery, and Romance: Formula Stories as Art and Popular Culture* (Chicago: University of Chicago Press, 1976), pp. 41–42.

sex, obsessive sex, and specifically a depiction of sexuality and sexual relations that affirms and maintains an ideology of female subordination and submission.[3] Whether these critics read the fictions of romance as merely erotic or as a form of outright pornography, they find in romance a fantasy literature that exploits female sexuality in the interest of the status quo, a retrograde vision of gender relations in which women submit to superior male force. Even the conventional romance resolution in marriage provides no triumph in this view—not for women and not for love—for in romance, marriage, like sex, conventionally valorizes a condition of permanent female dependency.

It is inarguable that romance publishers have found sexuality a popular and profitable subject. What popular literature for women once treated in a carefully coded system of allusions and evasions is now the central and essential material of this literature. Sexuality has become the discourse of popular romance. Still, what romance promises is love. And though it is tempting, because it is easy, to dismiss the claim of love as an example of the genteel code, as merely a euphemism for sex, it is more useful to take this claim at face value, at least conditionally, in order to determine just what it means.[4]

3. For example, Ann Douglas, in an important attack on Harlequin romances, labels them "soft-porn," an example of mass culture "specializ[ing] in dominance games, fantasies in which women lose and men win." Analyzing the romance formula, Douglas points out the focus on courtship, reduced to "coupling in the wary primitive modes of animal mating," which "crudely elaborate[s] the physiological and psychological condition of girls in love." Romance heroines experience a powerful sexual awakening early in the story so that "the emotional force of current Harlequin Romances comes from the brute energy of the male and the over-responsiveness of the female." Douglas argues that Harlequins "are porn softened to fit the needs of female emotionality," essentially, that is, "dramas of dependency" ("Soft-Porn Culture," *The New Republic* [30 August 1980]: 25–29).

Tania Modleski provides a considerably more insightful and balanced analysis. Although she sees romances as encouraging the reader "to participate in and actively desire feminine self-betrayal," she also identifies more aggressive elements in these stories, albeit carefully disguised (*Loving with a Vengeance: Mass-Produced Fantasies for Women* [Hamden, Conn.: Archon Books, 1982], p. 37).

4. Beatrice Faust has taken on the assignment of investigating male and female pornography and concludes that they are based on entirely different psychological responses and that female pornography is represented only in the *Sweet Savagery* type of bodice-ripper. But Faust's argument turns on the curious assumption that

If one accepts as significant the claims of both the publishers and the critics, it is possible to identify three key terms at issue: sex, love, and marriage. And if one examines closely the love story in popular romance, examines, that is, the surface story alone, ignoring for the present the coded story of power and appropriation, it becomes clear that these same terms represent the basic thematic elements on which that story turns. A dynamic trio of values emerges around which the conflict develops and resolves.

Sex, love, and marriage do not, however, signify experiences within any necessarily unified construct. The distinctions among physical, emotional, and contractual relations are thoroughly blurred by forcing them into conjunction. That, however, is pre-

pornography based on rape fantasies can be useful reading matter for women, offering "a certain guidance across the minefield of permissiveness, helping women find their bearings in the new sexual culture." Though these books avoid the important issues facing women at the present time, she writes, they serve an audience that itself prefers not to grapple with those issues. For that audience, bodice-rippers provide "a soft option. . . . The often raped but never ruined heroines provide surrogate experiences for women who have no intention of putting permissiveness to the test in real life" (*Women, Sex, and Pornography* [New York: Macmillan, 1980], p. 156).

Stephen Heath contends that the pornographic, as a nineteenth-century phenomenon, establishes a world in which "everything turns on the penis-phallus and the potential disturbance of its identity by the woman (as women are seen from its perspective, the opposite and mirroring pole to that of the man to which men are held.)" According to Heath, therefore, pornography is a generalized contemporary phenomenon, including the work of D. H. Lawrence on the one hand and that of sexology and psychoanalysis on the other (*The Sexual Fix* [London: Macmillan, 1982], pp. 106 and 108).

Ann Barr Snitow argues that Harlequin romances are pornographic, but claims that they develop a pornography keyed to the needs of women living in late capitalism and appealing to infantile narcissism. This pornography for women, she argues, is one in which "sex is bathed in romance, diffused, always implied rather than enacted at all" ("Mass Market Romance: Pornography for Women Is Different," *Powers of Desire*, ed. Ann Barr Snitow, Christine Stansell, and Sharon Thompson [New York: New Feminist Library, Monthly Review Press, 1983], pp. 245–63).

Janice Radway believes that for the romance readers she studied "sex is unalterably linked with the idea of romantic love." Her work with these readers leads her to conclude that their "feelings appear to be remarkably close to the erotic anticipation, excitement, and contentment prompted when any individual is the object of another's total attention. In effect, romance reading provides a vicarious experience of emotional nurturance *and* erotic anticipation and excitation" (*Reading the Romance*, pp. 104–5).

cisely the point. What must be kept in mind in a careful reading of popular romance is that it provides a fantasy solution to social conditions that are popularly accepted as insoluble. As fant' sy, romance fiction addresses and redresses gender relations across a range of social and economic issues, but the surface story of love specifically takes on the question of gender relations in the area of sexuality, and this is why it is necessarily played out through a narrative centered in sexuality ,through what I call the "sexual plot" in romance fiction   about love in the discourse of sexuality, and resolves that story through the convention, social and literary, of marriage. In the fantasy provided by the surface story in popular romance the conjunction of sex, love, and marriage is not only possible, it is logical and natural—and it is necessary.

The interaction among the key terms of sex, love, and marriage establishes the dynamics of popular romance in the sense that the basic conflict in the sexual plot pits them against one another in a series of dualisms: sex versus love, for example, or sex as free expression versus sex as the domain of married love; then, by extension, chastity versus sexual freedom, and sexual freedom versus marriage; ultimately male versus female. It is romance itself that mediates between these terms of opposition, finding their resolution. "Romance" in this formulation, however, is a multivalent term, pointing at one moment to romance as an idealized concept of sexual love and at the next to a particular kind of contemporary mass-market fiction, naming romance as fantasy, then romance as genre. It is also, in the terms Northrop Frye uses in *Anatomy of Criticism*, the "nearest of all literary forms to the wish-fulfillment dream."[5] In mediating between the dualisms established by the key terms of sex, love, and marriage, romance accomplishes a remarkable feat of wish-fulfillment, a gratification possible only in fantasy.

In *The Secular Scripture*, Frye extends his original discussion of literary romance to include popular literature, "what people read without guidance from their betters," and he observes that the "cen-

5. Northrop Frye, *Anatomy of Criticism* (Princeton, N.J.: Princeton University Press, 1957), p. 186.

tral element in romance is ⟨ ⟩ story" in which "the exciting
adventures are normally a f ⟨ ⟩ y leading up to sexual union."[6]
I argue that in the contemp ⟨ ⟩ romance formula the "exciting
adventures" are not metapho ⟨ ⟩ but literally a matter of sexual
foreplay and that the story c ⟨ ⟩ heroine's emotional life as she
meets the force of male sexual ⟨ ⟩ profitably be seen as the story
of her "adventures." As Frye n ⟨ ⟩ exual union provides the resolution, but in popular romanc ⟨ ⟩ al union, too, takes a specific
shape in the promise of marri ⟨ ⟩ it does not merely legitimize
sexual union but fundamentall ⟨ ⟩ morphoses it. My argument
rests, then, on the assumption that it is possible and useful to see
the romance heroine as the "hero" of a particularly contemporary
form of traditional romance, a form produced specifically to answer
the otherwise unanswerable questions posed by women as a subordinated class. Popular romance, from this point of view, is the story
of the heroine's quest.

The heroine's quest, like that of the traditional romance hero,
takes her into a privileged space, one freed of much of the machin-
ery and paraphernalia of the "real world." Despite the trappings
of realistic fiction adopted by popular romance, these stories take
place outside of a dense social matrix,[7] as if deliberately to deny the
other, coded story of power relations under real social conditions.
The importance of the asocial space set aside for the romance love
story is that, unlike the love story in the comic tradition, romance
shows no interest in imposing social constraints on young love. No
problems of family opposition or of real or imagined class differ-

---

6. Northrop Frye, *The Secular Scripture: A Study of the Structure of Romance* (Cambridge: Harvard University Press, 1982), p. 24.

7. Reflexes of realism in romance can be seen in the careful establishment of a
contemporary world, figured essentially in the identification of setting as an actual
place, typically urban, and in the elaborate descriptions of high-priced consumer
goods, especially clothes and cars. Moreover, romance fiction, as it is produced
for Harlequin and similar publishers, resolutely avoids any "unrealistic" effects; no
Gothic elements intrude. Realism in romance fiction may do little more than affect
a posture, but the posture is important, suggesting that there is nothing magical in
the heroine's story, that it can happen to anyone.

For a full discussion of the uses of mimesis in romance narrative, see Radway,
Reading the Romance, pp. 186–208.

ence prevent the hero and heroine from loving and marrying at the outset. In the absence of such obstacles, romance fiction sets itself the task of developing its own kind of narrative progression, its own set of problems and strategies to keep the lovers apart until the story closes. Therefore, rather than a story of love's victory over socially imposed obstacles, the sexual plot in popular romance tells a story of discovery, of the uncovering of a powerful secret, of the triumphant acquisition of love as a hermetic truth. The question popular romance poses is not "Will the lovers win?" but "Will the lovers *know?*"

Hero and heroine alike must discover that they love, but because the story of romance is the story of the romance heroine, the problem of attaining knowledge is essentially hers. She must discover that she loves, and in contemporary romance that discovery must come through the agency of sexuality. Sexuality in romance fiction carries enormous significance, a significance that becomes plain only through a careful analysis of the sexual material itself and through a consideration of the sexual plot in romance fiction in terms of its affinities to literary romance.

The important issue about sexuality in romance is not its moral or aesthetic or political value, nor the absence of these, but its absolute centrality. Sexuality is the *res gestae* of romance, the stuff out of which the story is made. If one eliminates the sexual material, the story line remaining is entirely rudimentary. There are three unvarying segments: an initial meeting between the hero and heroine, which incurs the heroine's hostility to the hero; a long period of armed truce during which the hero and heroine are thrown together typically to work toward some mutually accepted goal; and a final episode of danger, rescue, and exile leading to the declaration of love.

Much more developed than the skeletal story line is the sexual plot, itself unvarying, which weaves through these segments to give the story its narrative substance. The sexual plot, in fact, is consistent even in those more recent romances that feature sexual consummation rather than merely sexual arousal. These romances will be investigated in a later chapter; the significant point for the present is that the *degree* of sexual intimacy between the hero and the heroine in no way alters the shape or the meaning of the sexual plot.

Thus, the initial meeting forces on the heroine a new sexual self-consciousness, which accounts for her hostility toward the hero. The period of uneasy truce and of proximity between the hero and heroine is marked by encounters of increasingly intense sexuality; the hero's advances grow more charged and aggressive, and the heroine's responses force on her a recognition of her own urgently sexual self. The concluding episode of danger, rescue, and exile alters the hero's behavior, substituting for sexuality the expression of warmth and tenderness, characteristics associated with love. Because the formulaic elements of the story and the formulaic elements of the sexual plot work hand in hand, the erotic aspect of romance is greatly highlighted. Sexuality is not one element among several; nor is it a narrative "extra," an extrinsic reward for the prurient reader. What romance narrates *is* the progress of the erotic.

Within the formulaic structures of story line and sexual plot, the romance heroine undertakes her quest, but the constraints and strictures of both romance formula and bourgeois fiction inhibit the heroine, making her a kind of romance hero manqué. Like that hero, she is engaged in a quest, but unlike him she must maintain her ignorance not only of the object of the quest but of the very fact that she is questing. The romance heroine is in search of love, in its conventionalized form as marriage, but she is no freer from the immutable laws of bourgeois fiction than other heroines of that tradition; like them she is virtuously constrained from acknowledging or even recognizing that this is her goal. Again like the romance hero, she is an innocent abroad in a hostile landscape. But the landscape of popular romance is internal, the adventure psychological, and the heroine's innocence altogether a sexual innocence. Finally the romance heroine, like the hero of romance, confronts and battles her antagonist, meeting him in a "crucial struggle," in Frye's terms, "some kind of battle in which either the hero or his foe, or both, must die."[8] But for the romance heroine the antagonist and the

8. Frye, *Anatomy of Criticism*, p. 187.

21

object of the quest are one: the hero assumes both roles. Nor is this a simple matter of disguise, the hero finally laying aside an assumed antagonistic role to reappear as true prince. On the contrary, a battle is engaged and the antagonist bested: the heroine succeeds in expurgating, in killing off, the hero's threatening sexuality, the aspect of him that imperils her. Such is the triumph of love.

Popular romance operates within the broad frame of literary romance, but it is a diminished and claustrophobic form of romance, for it is enacted entirely on the field of sexuality; no larger vision intrudes. Since sexuality altogether imbues romance, it is essential that the erotics of romance be explicated through an analysis of the key moments of sexual conflict and discovery.

One of the problems in reading formula fiction is the temptation to accept as given what the formula presents as given. That temptation must be avoided even at the expense of questioning the apparently obvious. Popular romance, for example, opens with the instant establishment of hostility between heroine and hero and the concomitant awareness on the heroine's part of the hero's sexual appeal. As an unvarying element of formula, the conjunction of attraction and hostility takes on a sense of naturalness, of the expected and therefore the obvious, even of the "realistic." But of course that is not the case. Romance insists on an illogical conjunction, and this requires some examination.

Certainly, hostility serves the plot: it is necessary to postpone the happy ending in order to have any story to tell. But the attraction-hostility conjunction is essential in another way as well; since romance has rejected traditional social obstacles to love, it must implant the conflict internally from the outset. Insofar as a heroine and hero meet and take a mutual dislike to one another, a dislike that is eventually transmuted into love, romance merely follows an established pattern. Moreover, such a tactic, as in *Pride and Prejudice*, defends the heroine against the charge of seeking love and marriage, especially to a wealthy man. But popular romance differs from this familiar fictional pattern in making it both explicit and necessary that the heroine's hostility be an automatic reaction to sexual attraction. The heroine may be sexually innocent, but she is innately, instinctively aware that sexuality menaces her.

22

Some romances do attempt to rationalize the heroine's initial hostility to the hero by adding a secondary, nonsexual motivation. A minor car accident, a difficult employer-employee relationship, or a simple misunderstanding serves to initiate unfriendly relations. Other stories omit such extrasexual motivation, allowing sexual peril to carry its own defensive response in hostility. A good example is Amii Lorin's *Morgan Wade's Woman*, where the rapid stages of attraction, response, fear, and hostility occur without any attempt to rationalize or motivate them beyond the bare fact of sexuality. Meeting Morgan Wade, the heroine, Samantha Denning, instantly responds: "Feeling the short hairs on her nape bristle, Sam thought, *That's the most dangerous-looking male animal I've ever seen.* On the heels of that thought she felt a tiny curl in her stomach which she recognized, in some shock, as fear." Puzzled, even amazed, at her reaction, Samantha thinks that "It was almost as if, in some way, he was a threat to her." The requisite defensive strategy occurs at once: "a slow anger beginning to burn inside." Their eyes meet and a challenge is given and accepted, "warfare silently declared."[9] Scarcely a word has been exchanged between hero and heroine, but the dynamics of their relationship are established as sexual warfare.

Formulaic expectations alone give this scene meaning. Wade Morgan has done nothing to elicit such a response; introduced to Samantha at the home of friends, he behaves with perfect decorum. Only his eyes, as the heroine reads them, express any challenge. Certainly, not all romance heroes are so well mannered. Often they offer patronizing comments and domineering sexual gestures in their first meeting with the heroine. But the heroine's confused response of attraction and hostility typically precedes any actions at all on the part of the hero; his actions serve only to intensify her initial response.

The hero is, at the outset, much less the sum of what he says or does than simply the physical expression of male sexual energy. Often his physical presence alone is adequate expression of that energy. One heroine sees the hero appear, silent, but with "the air of

9. Amii Lorin, *Morgan Wade's Woman* (New York: Dell, Candlelight Ecstasy Romance, 1981), pp. 34–35.

raw, primordial bearing emanating from him." [10] Another first meets the hero in the dark; with only his voice to characterize him, he emits "vibrations of mastery and mystery." [11] In one case, so compelling and alluring is the hero, that the heroine falls under the sexual spell of his picture before she ever meets him: "She stood before his portrait, transfixed, immobilized by luminous eyes that were black as chips of coal. They burned into the depths of her being with relentless fury." [12]

Although a good deal has been made of the aggressive quality of male sexuality in romance, it is, in fact, the heroine's own erotic response and not the hero's real or perceived brutality that arouses her deepest fears and elicits her hostile reaction. Romance heroes are sometimes violent and brutal, nearly always arrogant, occasionally tender and empathic. None of this alters the formulaic course of the heroine's terror and anger. The criticism of romance fiction that points to the depiction of male sexuality as violent and even rapelike correctly observes a pervasive element of romance, but fails to understand its function. It is not a question of a pornography of rape-fantasy or an erotics of violence; rather, it is a simple, an elementary way of realizing in character and action the violent danger that sexuality in the abstract is understood as posing. [13]

10. Paula Edwards, *Bewitching Grace* (New York: Simon and Schuster, Silhouette Romances, 1980), p. 12.

11. Violet Winspear, *A Girl Possessed* (New York: Harlequin Books, 1980), p. 11.

12. Patti Beckman, *Angry Lover* (New York: Simon and Schuster, Silhouette Books, 1981), p. 34.

13. While some feminist critics have merely excoriated what they read as gratuitous male brutality in romance, more careful examinations of romance strategies have led to more complex interpretations. Tania Modleski, for example, argues that the violent expression of male sexuality plays a role in romance fiction because the heroine is taxed with the problem of learning to understand it: "It is the function of the novels to explain such brutality in a lover," she explains. "Male brutality comes to be seen as a manifestation not of contempt, but of love" (*Loving with a Vengeance*, pp. 39–41).

Janice Radway studies a group of romance readers and finds that stories with excessive violence are never favored. Stories considered to be "good" romances are those in which male violence is not only controlled but also in the end unmasked as a defensive posture. "In good romances, the overly aggressive masculine behavior is exposed as a false or defensive facade that, when removed, as it inevitably is, reveals the true male personality to be kind and tender." Like Modleski, then,

The dangers of sexuality are multiple. First, sexuality enters the lives of romance heroines as an alien experience, the province of the hero, the expression of his threatening potency. The fact that the heroine responds to that potency utterly imperils her selfhood. Her will is threatened; her self-mastery jeopardized. Moreover, the heroine's own body betrays her, becomes itself the enemy. It is as if the play of erotic emotions brings about the existence of a new and alien being within the heroine's own person, a being that would participate in her betrayal. Awakened to sexuality, eroticism internalized, the heroine is threatened from within and without.

The intensifying erotic conflict that makes up the greatest part of the material in popular romance is internalized, for eroticism in romance is psychological rather than physical, a matter of what the heroine is experiencing emotionally. An important index to internal and emotional eroticism in contrast to an externalized and physical sexual emphasis lies in the language of popular romance. The descriptions of sexual episodes are largely explorations of the heroine's feelings rather than depictions of physical activities; consequently, romance writers typically reach for high-flown, often tortured attempts at erotic metaphor.[14]

Embedded in the unobtrusive, pedestrian narrative of romance, the language of emotional eroticism, no matter how excessive, plays an important role. By heightening passages in the sexual plot, language itself becomes erotic, an instrument of seduction. The hero's

Radway sees masculine aggression as something that needs to be interpreted, but the interpretation that romances supply tells its readers that this behavior "implies only good things for women. It is the sign of sexual difference and thus a fundamental condition for the love, marriage, and attention women seek." From this point of view, Radway suggests, it is possible to understand that romance writers—and by extension, romance readers—are engaged not in exercises in masochism but in attempts to respond to "a desperate need to know that exaggerated masculinity is not life-threatening to women" (*Reading the Romance*, p. 168).

14. In part, avoiding explicit physical sexuality is enforced by romance publishers who find explicit sex unacceptable. Without doubt, such a policy conforms to the tastes of genteel readers. Recently, readers' tastes have changed to the extent that many accept less genteel and rather more explicit sexuality. Romance publishers, always intensely responsive to the market, manage to meet the needs of a wide range of readers by publishing different series of romance stories, the degree of sexuality signaled by the series' names as well as by the cover illustrations.

words much more than his actions carry the force of his sexual potency. They are intended to inflame. One hero threatens to " 'kiss you into submission, teach you delights that would make you gasp and swoon, make love to you for hours, and carry you from one mountaintop after another of fulfillment.' " [15] Another promises that " 'Some day, my silken-skinned Rosa with the golden hair, we will write *conciertos* together on the galaxies and I shall play you as I play my guitar.' " [16]

Erotic language also names romance heroes. Heroines, in their roles as everywoman, often have commonplace names: Lin Blake or Rosie Powell or Ann Milan. Even when their names are less ordinary, like Samantha Denning or Deborah Denhoff, they are no match for those of the heroes: Joshua Revell, Bayne Dahlquist, Derek Veblen, Adam Noble, Soren Wingard, Anton DeVere, Eric Damon.[17] The heroes are named extravagantly, as if even the language that serves to identify them identifies as well and partakes of the exotic and sensual. The linguistic power associated with romance heroes reinforces male potency at the level of language itself, a reflex of male dominance.

Enmeshed in a world and a discourse thick with sensuality, the heroine faces a conflict drawn along two lines: the heroine struggles against the sexual potency of the hero, which threatens to subdue and dominate her; at the same time, her own new erotic response enters combat with her intellect. In crudely psychoanalytic terms, ego and id struggle for supremacy, but romance writers avoid these terms. In crudely moralistic terms, the heroine fights to maintain her chastity, but chastity in itself lacks dramatic power as a sign. The heroine of romance believes that sexual consummation belongs properly to the married state, but as Northrop Frye suggests, "the social reasons for the emphasis on virginity, however obvious, are

15. Beckman, *Angry Lover*, p. 81.

16. Susanna Collins, *Flamenco Nights* (New York: Jove Books, Second Chance at Love, 1981), p. 29.

17. Occasionally a romance writer, while naming her heroines very conservatively, will assume for herself a particularly extravagant pseudonym. A striking and particularly aggressive example is Violet Winspear.

still not enough for understanding the structures of romance."[18] The sexual conflict is fought out in its own terms.

Male sexuality endangers not only the heroine's body but her will. In part this is no more than a euphemism, a gloss on the Victorian phrase, "He had his will of her," and as such reduces the heroine's will simply to her will to resist, to preserve herself chaste. But in part it indicates a more thoroughgoing dominance, an expunging of the heroine's selfhood. Often an erotic passage will slide from one meaning to another: "But this was no lover's kiss, given and returned in tenderness. It was a practiced assault on her senses, intended deliberately to reduce her to absolute submission to his will. . . . And it was succeeding. She could feel herself weakening and the fight going out of her. . . . She was fighting a losing battle, clinging desperately to the last rags of her self-control."[19]

Though the obsessive emphasis on submission in romance fiction has a good deal to do with the male sexuality as violent and brutal, the significant issue here is the import of sexual violence within the structure of the sexual plot and in the dynamics of the conflict. As I noted earlier, the depiction, or threat, of male violence makes real in romance the abstract power of sexuality itself. At the same time, such imminent danger intensifies the adventure of the heroine and enhances the value of her final victory. The erotic component of romance, instinct with violence, is what the heroine must deal with. In her romantic adventure, sexuality plays the role of giants and dragons, witchcraft and enchantments.

The problem for contemporary popular romance, on the level of the sexual plot, is to manage and contain the sexuality the heroine discovers and to turn that sexuality into an instrument in the service of love. This is a difficult task precisely because sexuality blossoms within the heroine; it is no longer an aspect only of the threatening other but a new part of her own being. As one romance heroine expresses this, "It was not his attempt to make love to her which had scared her rigid; it was her own secret desire to have him make love

18. Frye, *The Secular Scripture*, p. 73.
19. Sally Wentworth, *Liberated Lady* (New York: Harlequin Books, 1979), p. 103.

to her."[20] Against this traitor within, the heroine has only her "better self": "While her brain fought a desperate battle to keep control of her body and to reject him, her senses clamoured treacherously for the touch of his lips on hers."[21] Sexuality, the hero's and her own, now has the heroine entirely in thrall.

The strategy of romance fiction is not to reject sexuality out of hand but to turn this alien power to the service of love triumphant. Three tactics are instrumental in accomplishing this. First, the new sexuality within the heroine takes on a special value as the sign of her womanliness. Second, the heroine's sexual response to the hero becomes the evidence of her love for him. And third, male sexuality, at first seen as entirely dissociated from love, is transmuted and domesticated into a new, love-evidencing sexuality. Each of these tactics requires discussion.

First, sexual arousal in romance signals the beginning of the heroine's entrance into womanhood. Before this happens, she is immature, incomplete. Although the subject of the romance heroine's initiation into womanhood will be taken up in another chapter, it is important to point out here that the heroine's experience in suffering the betrayal of her own body is a necessary part of that initiation. Until that is accomplished, she remains a girl, even a child—sometimes an adorable child, "a little wisp of an innocent barely out of the schoolroom,"[22] sometimes a spoiled and willful child who "lacks the guts to grow up" and continues "behaving like a very spoiled little girl."[23] The heroine's acknowledgment and understanding of her own sexuality leads her along the route from childhood to womanhood.

The next stage brings a full understanding of female sexuality for the romance heroine, who now recognizes that sexuality and love are one—for women. Insofar as popular romance is an adventure of discovery, this is the heroine's crucial discovery, but her new knowledge brings neither happiness nor power. Sexual responsiveness

20. Charlotte Lamb, *Retribution* (New York: Harlequin Books, 1981), p. 114.
21. Suzanna Firth, *Dark Encounter* (New York: Harlequin Books, 1979), p. 91.
22. Suzanne Simmons, *The Tempestuous Lovers* (New York: Dell, A Candlelight Ecstasy Romance, 1981), p. 74.
23. Lorin, *Morgan Wade's Woman*, pp. 80, 113.

had threatened submission to male dominance; now love promises worse, for love is understood, mysteriously, as the ultimate secret, which, if revealed, places the heroine in peril of a shameful dependency. The heroine of romance who finds herself, midway in the story, in love, is at the nadir of her adventure.

The romance heroine, conventional girl that she is, has been taught that sexual desire and love are entirely distinct. "'Wanting,'" one heroine "primly" informs the hero, "'should never be confused with loving.'"[24] Another, recalling the erotic pleasures she has shared with the hero, wonders "where was the line between raw sexual desire and love? The intoxicating moments she dreamed about, relived breathlessly, were all things she had been taught were not for a decent girl's mind. . . . And yet those fevered hours with Juan seemed only the most beautiful outpourings of her love."[25] Convinced at last that her sexual response is in fact the evidence of love, the heroine despairs. "She gave in to fresh sobs, realizing perhaps for the first time, how deeply she had fallen in love with him."[26] "No, she didn't want to love him, yet she faced the fact that she was his. She did love him. She wept silently."[27] But the heroine's course is soon clear; at all costs she must conceal her love from the hero, for love leaves her altogether vulnerable: "Now that she faced the truth at last, that she was in love with Clement, she had no defenses left that she could rely upon."[28]

The formulaic discovery that the heroine's sexual response to the hero proves her love for him is critical to the strategies of romance fiction. For one thing, it provides an a posteriori moral alibi for her earlier eroticism; her response to the hero was, after all, a response out of love. More important, it enlists sexuality under the banner of love, subduing sex itself to the ends of love. Female sexuality, though it may have been elicited by male sexuality, has its own character as handmaiden to love. The heroine, at first the victim of

24. Flora Kidd, *A Personal Affair* (New York: Harlequin Books, 1981), p. 154.

25. Collins, *Flamenco Nights*, p. 111.

26. Tracy Adams, *The Moth and the Flame* (New York: Simon and Schuster, Silhouette Books, 1981), p. 68.

27. Lorin, *Morgan Wade's Woman*, p. 77.

28. Beckman, *Angry Lover*, p. 142.

male potency, becomes instead the victim of love. Since love is, for the present, unrequited, the heroine's suffering is not alleviated; in fact, it increases. But the important issue is that the terms of the heroine's conflict have shifted from sexuality to love, that sexuality has been brought under the dominion of love.

The distinction between male and female sexuality in the paradigms of romance fiction lies in the fact that male sexuality is understood as being, or as believing itself, free of love. As such, male sexuality is the expression of independence, of a generalized sense of a libertinism that is liberty. Such a paradigm might lead to the despairing belief that the struggle between the sexes can come to no resolution, that man and woman are at once joined and permanently separated through the agency of sexuality. Romance, however, in the culmination of its strategy for reconstructing sexuality, provides its fantasy solution: it becomes the heroine's task to remake male sexuality, to subordinate it, too, to love.

From one point of view, and in the long tradition established by Richardson's *Pamela*, all this rhetoric of love might be dismissed as a banal disguise for the heroine's merely holding out for marriage. Some support for this point of view comes in the fact that most romances present as practically simultaneous the declaration of the hero's love and his proposal of marriage. In fact, the two declarations serve very different functions.

The essential function of the marriage proposal in popular romance is to provide closure, but as a form of narrative resolution the marriage proposal moves the story out of the romance tradition and allies it loosely to the tradition of comedy. By bringing the lovers together in marriage, romance borrows its resolution from the literary tradition that bases the plot of a love story on the hero's and heroine's ability to overcome the obstacles to their love imposed by society—obstacles such as parental objections or class difference. The comic resolution that brings the lovers to victory over those obstacles celebrates love and youth and at the same time promises an end to social disruption, for the marriage of the lovers signals their absorption into the social fabric and provides the comic promise of continuity within the now-harmonious social world. But the romance story, existing apart from a dense social matrix, does not

30

base its conflict on the antagonism between the lovers and society. For that reason, the marriage proposal in romance lacks the resonance it has in comedy, representing simply a convenient form of fictional resolution along with a polite acknowledgment of conventional mores and values.

Not that the promise of marriage is without meaning in contemporary romance; but given the dynamics of romance formula, it pales in significance before the power of the hero's avowal of love. Marriage is conventionally required, but it is not at all emotionally adequate to effect the resolution of the love story. A popular variant of the romance formula makes this point emphatically. In this version the hero and heroine are married early in the story, some more or less improbable pretext serving as motive. The early marriage variant has the advantage of allowing sexual consummation under the banner of marital legitimacy, but this in no way alters the pattern of the heroine's emotional adventures. Despite the fact of marriage, love and sex remain the terms under which the conflict is carried out and the resolution accomplished.

Marriage, as this variant form tells us, legitimizes sexual relations, but it is only love that makes sex meaningful and fulfilling. The heroine of romance typically defends herself against sex by calling on love—not marriage—as a necessary precondition to consummation, and when she does invoke marriage, a much rarer occurrence, it is as a state itself predicated on love. The romance hero, moreover, not only avoids marriage in the interests of preserving his liberty; more crucially, in his unregenerate state he is an avowed disbeliever in love. As one hero puts it, " 'Love is an illusion. . . . And I am above all a realist.' "[29]

Because he does not believe in love, the romance hero cannot understand that it is the absence of love that makes the heroine resist his attempts at seduction; as a result he chalks it up to a Pamela-like shrewdness, accusing the heroine of bartering her body for marriage. " 'I'd have to love a man before I slept with him,' " declares one heroine. But the hero ignores the word "love," replying, " 'Any man that wants you has to be prepared to make the ultimate ges-

29. Simmons, *The Tempestuous Lovers*, p. 109.

ture of offering you marriage.'"[30] This is the most damaging of all accusations in romance, for it carries with it overtones of economic and sexual calculation. Another hero makes this point in bluntly economic terms. "'I can see which one of us is the cold-blooded merchant here. I have a deep feeling for you, a need as old as the human race for us to be together. But you have with great shrewdness put a price tag on your virginity. You are up for sale—and the price tag is a marriage license and a wedding ring!'"[31] He, too, will capitulate once he has said the magic word "love"; an evasive periphrasis like "deep feeling" will not suffice.

The proposal of marriage belongs to the tradition of comedy, but the declaration of love comes properly from romance. Up to the point of resolution, when love is declared, the heroine has despaired of the hero's love, assured that for him sexual desire exists independently of love: "He hadn't mentioned love. He had talked of need, but not of love."[32] "He would grow tired of trying to prove that he wanted her. But desire wasn't love. Not once had he said he loved her."[33] The knowledge of her own love is accessible to the heroine, a discovery she can make. She cannot, however, learn by herself of the hero's love; that love must be announced, and it is, in fact, the saying that matters, the speaking of the word. No romance hero, moreover, whatever offenses might be laid to him, ever speaks the word "love" in vain. Nor, once said, can love be withdrawn; nor will it ever alter. With the resonance of ritual, the word "love" is uttered at the denouement of every romance.

"I love you," he said quietly and suddenly, and surprise robbed her of breath."[34]

"God, Nicki, don't you know the hell you've put me through? Can't you see that I'm hopelessly, desperately, out of my mind with love for you?"[35]

30. Firth, *Dark Encounter*, p. 93.
31. Beckman, *Angry Lover*, p. 176.
32. Lamb, *Retribution*, p. 160.
33. Adams, *The Moth and the Flame*, p. 155.
34. Kidd, *A Personal Affair*, p. 182.
35. Simmons, *The Tempestuous Lovers*, p. 185.

32

"Hate you?" he grated. "You redheaded witch, I love you."[36]

"I do love you, you know. Have loved you, I think, from the first moment I laid eyes on you."[37]

The formulaic, even ritualized significance of the declaration of love cannot be exaggerated. "Declaration," in fact, is an inadequate term; it is as confession, as something wrung from the hero, that love is spoken. A ceremonial, even an incantatory word, "love" brings with it the profound and permanent metamorphosis into union toward which the story has inexorably driven. The speaking aloud of a word heretofore spoken, if at all, in derisive irony represents more than the necessary rounding off of a formulaic convention. The naming of love stands at the heart of the ritual that popular romance reenacts for its readers.

But even the confession of love in itself does not quite suffice to complete the work of romance. It is necessary as well that the hero's long struggle against love be made clear. He has loved long and in silence, a silence, moreover, that represents his allegiance to some other powerful force, a masculine principle of sexuality whose very potency depends on its freedom from commitment. The hero, then, like the heroine, has experienced conflict, has been caught in a struggle between two powerful forces until at last he surrenders to the stronger force, to the heroine and to love. As one transformed hero expresses it: " 'I love you, Tiana. It goes against the philosophy I adopted for myself, but so help me, I do love you. . . . When I met you, I no longer believed in the abstract concept of love. . . . Yet from the moment I first saw you, I was drawn to you. . . . I tried to convince myself that if I could just possess you, have an affair with you, I would get it out of my system. But it never seemed to work because I already loved you so much."[38] Male sexuality, unlike female sexuality, is not the seedbed of love, but, in its redeemed form, it becomes the servant of love. Women, romance tells us, learn love through eroticism; men's potency, conversely, is tamed under the sway of love.

36. Lorin, *Morgan Wade's Woman*, p. 173.
37. Beckman, *Angry Lover*, p. 186.
38. Edwards, *Bewitching Grace*, pp. 186–87.

The conflict between the hero and the heroine of popular romance and the internalized conflict the heroine undergoes at the emergence of her own sexual being are both resolved in the concluding triumph of love. In its more benign message, romance promises the legitimation of passion in love and, consequently, marriage between loving and equal partners. In a darker tone, romance celebrates a more thoroughgoing female victory at the expense of the defeated and diminished male.

The complex and ambiguous resolution of the sexual plot derives from the double role assigned the romance hero, at once the antagonist in the heroine's adventure and the goal of her quest. The romance heroine seeks love, but in her adventure the heroine meets not love but lust, sexual passion expressed and represented by the hero, her antagonist and outspoken disbeliever in "the abstract concept of love." In his role as enemy, the hero tries to seduce the heroine. This is not simply a question of illicit sexuality, but of deflecting the heroine from her true quest. In a less economic fiction where a fuller cast of characters is developed, the heroine might well elude the seducer to find her true love in another person. But contemporary popular romance does not care for that solution. The point of contemporary popular romance is precisely that the antagonist and the object of the quest are one, the male at once dangerous and desired. The heroine, therefore, is not charged with the straightforward task of rejecting the seducer in favor of the lover; instead, her ordeal consists in remaking the seducer, turning him into lover and husband.

The victory of love over sexuality lies at the heart of the strategies romance has devised for providing a fantasy of female victory. Whatever secondary rewards the pleasures of the erotic may provide the romance reader, the sexual discourse and the sexual plot of popular romance serve a far more serious purpose. The foregrounding of sexual material in contemporary romance in itself points to the fact that sexuality is seen as difficult and problematic, that it is an area in women's lives where fantasy resolutions are required in the absence of real solutions under existing social conditions.

Romance is produced for an audience that is, generally speaking, profoundly conservative. It is not intended to serve either the "sexu-

34

ally liberated" woman or the radical feminist who attacks the conventional gender relations that lie at the very root of basic cultural assumptions and constructs. Therefore, contemporary romance fiction does not directly challenge popular assumptions about male-female sexual relations; it provides no new ideology. Its strategies are designed to operate within conventional attitudes and beliefs, but to manage and manipulate them in the service of a fantasy that asserts the victory of women over men, of love triumphant, and to do so specifically through a sexual discourse and a sexual plot.

The severely limited political agenda of romance fiction means that its fantasy gratification in romance operates psychologically rather than socially. It is the individual reader alone whose condition is ameliorated, whose life is improved—if only fantastically, vicariously, and temporarily. That there are millions of these individual readers makes no difference, for there is no appeal made to the aggregate, no gesture made toward revolutionary change. The very world of the romance novel inhibits such response; it is a world as devoid of society and social relations as is possible, given the minimal reflexes of realism necessary to the formula.

In *The Sexual Fix*, Stephen Heath makes the point that "a characteristic of the kind of society in which we live is the mass production of fictions." He calls ours the culture of the "novelistic," marked by "the constant narration of the social relations of individuals, the ordering of meanings for the individuals in society." For Heath, the obsessive burden of this narration is the "fabrication of 'sexuality,'" the commodification of a phallocentric sexuality in which woman remains both object and other. The ideology of sexuality reduces selfhood to sexuality, makes "self-knowledge . . . sex"; "sex is how you know who you are, your real identity."[39]

Popular romance, as culturally determined as sexuality itself, participates in this narrative of sexuality, but tells its own version. Because romance does not challenge basic assumptions, it accepts the idea of selfhood as sexual. The romance heroine becomes fully herself, realizes her potential as woman, through the sexual awakening the romance hero elicits in her. This is at the very heart of

39. Heath, *The Sexual Fix*, p. 85.

35

sexual ideology, of course—as the resolution of romance fiction in the promise of loving marriage is at the heart of bourgeois ideology about women and the family. It is not here that fantasy gratification lies.

Only a careful examination of the sexual plot in romance allows us to see how romance maneuvers the mine field of sexuality. The critical, and ambiguous, aspect of the sexual discourse of romance is that though it accepts the phallocentric ideology of sexuality, it tells its story from the point of view of the heroine. That in itself is not new; *Fanny Hill*, to cite a key example, goes back two hundred years. But the heroine of popular romance is not objectified in the way that Cleland's heroine is, not conceived as a commodity whose particular charm lies in her eager participation in her own commodification, not conceived, that is, as a male fantasy.

Romance is female fantasy, but female fantasy within the confines of conservative ideology. Romance fictions leave in place the essential structure of sexual ideology, but they make critical adjustments to that structure, adjustments that, if only in fantasy, redistribute power in the sexual relations between men and women. More precisely, the sexual plot of popular romance reverses actual power relations by reducing them to the sexual relations between one particular woman and one particular man, between heroine and hero alone. The heroine's victory is personal, unique, and in its uniqueness makes no overt attack on existing conditions. In part, the heroine's victory is precisely her reward for good behavior, but this, once again, points only to the fundamental sexual conservatism of romance.

Conservative as it may be, popular romance, in its strategies for mediating between sex and love, provides a challenge and corrective to the centuries-old conception of sexual woman as menacing, as a devouring and insatiable monster. Nor does romance replace her with the icy virgin. The romance heroine may be virginal, but her potential womanliness is demonstrated by her erotic response to male sexuality. She is neither monster nor permanent maiden, but a heroine who succeeds in her task of mastering and managing passion, both her own and the hero's. The sexual discourse of romance may reverberate with violence and the sexual plot make its way through accepted strictures of ideology, but the terms by which that plot comes to resolution provide one of Western literature's rare defenses of female sexuality since Moll Flanders settled down to respectability.

2

THE ROMANCE HERO

Had he been a handsome, heroic-looking gentleman,
I should not have dared to stand thus
questioning him against his will,
and offering my services unasked.

Charlotte Brontë, *Jane Eyre*

$\mathscr{R}$omance fiction tells the story of the heroine and to that extent romance is *about* the heroine. But the dominant character in contemporary romance is always the hero. In the character of the hero inhere the excitement, the glamour, and the power of the desired. The surface story of romance narrates the heroine's success in winning and taming the object of sexual and romantic desire. The encoded story recounts her success in winning, in fact appropriating, the object of economic desire. The key to the contemporary romance hero lies in how the sexual and the economic have become fused, creating a tense and ambiguous pairing of mutually referential signs. Sexual power *means* economic power; economic power *means* sexual power. Nevertheless, there is no natural or necessary tie between economic power and sexual power. Their linking has come about historically; it is part of bourgeois ideology. Later chapters will consider the underlying historical conditions; first, we need a closer look at the romance hero as contemporary romance has constructed him.

The contemporary romance hero is a fantasy construct that is rooted in real social conditions. For romance readers he represents the satisfaction of all those desires that our culture both fosters and disappoints for women. Our culture values individualism, success, money, power, but has traditionally granted only to men the right to pursue them. And it values, even overvalues, romantic love, making it especially the province of women, instilling in them wildly improbable dreams of conjugal bliss.[1] Romance satisfies—as it feeds—

---

1. A number of historians have noted that the changing conception of marriage as the locus for romantic love has led to an overvaluation of love and the identification of love as a particularly female expression. Mary P. Ryan states that "the sentiment of love lost its equilibrium in the fashionable literature of the eighteenth century as the balance of conjugal affection tilted awkwardly toward the female" (*Womanhood in America: From Colonial Times to the Present*, 3d ed. [New York: Franklin Watts, 1983], pp. 91–92). See also Lawrence Stone, *The Family, Sex and Marriage* (New York: Harper and Row, 1977); Philippe Aries, "Love in Married Life," in *Western Sexuality: Practice and Precept in Past and Present Times*, ed. Philippe Aries and André Bejin, trans. Anthony Foster (London: Basil Blackwell, 1986); Carl Degler, *At Odds:*

the forbidden desire for male power and the unrealistic desire for female love, and it satisfies them both in the gorgeous figure of the hero.

For all his glamour, the hero of contemporary romance remains a type, a bundle of formulaic attributes on which only the most minimal changes are rung. So constant and so salient are these attributes that they can be reduced to a recipe, a set of guidelines. Here, for example, is the description of the hero as provided to would-be romance writers by Silhouette Books a number of years ago:

> The hero is 8 to 12 years older than the heroine. He is self-assured, masterful, hot-tempered, capable of violence, passion and tenderness. He is often mysteriously moody. . . . Always older than the heroine, usually in his early or late 30's, he is rich and successful in the vocation of his choice. . . . He is always tall, muscular (but not muscle-bound) with craggy features. He is not necessarily handsome, but is, above all, virile. He is usually dark.[2]

The guidelines emphasize superiority and dominance. The overdetermined insistence on age, the necessity of economic success, the stress placed on height and muscularity all imply a heroine who is inferior: younger, poorer, smaller, weaker. Along with dominance, the stress falls on mood, on the hero's capacity for "violence, passion and tenderness." Arbitrary shifts of behavior, moreover, are directly linked with social and economic dominance; such behavior, in fact, *is* the expression of dominance. Since the hero's moods are preeminently based in his sexual response to and pursuit of the heroine, it becomes apparent once again that sexuality serves to express the hero's generalized dominance and power.

But sexuality is never divorced from economic power, so romance writers must establish an economic context for their heroes, fit them out with a line of work, a chosen vocation in which they have become "rich and successful." But putting the hero to work is not a

Women and the Family in America from the Revolution to the Present (New York: Oxford University Press, 1980).

2. Undated, mimeographed guidelines from Silhouette Books.

simple matter. O   side lie all the cultural values inhering in
male work and m   cess; on the other, the ways in which work
threatens the fanta   olution of romance fiction, which promises
the heroine a full-t   isband and lover.

The hero's worl   ies his male energy and power; it is challenging, difficult, a   gle against odds, a battle against competition. Work is itself   As one might expect, the rags-to-riches
theme occurs frequ   evidencing the hero's ambition and drive,
and thereby his viri   f one hero we learn that "'He grew up in
an orphanage that he hated so much that he ran away when he was
only fourteen. He has survived by his wits alone in a cold world
where only the fittest survive.'"[3]

At the same time and despite all marketplace provocation, the
hero cannot be tarnished in any way at all by his success; not even
indirectly can he be seen as exploiting labor, polluting the environment, or trafficking with shady characters. Romance may be out to
redistribute power in its fantasy challenge to the bourgeois marketplace, but no reservations about the marketplace can be reflected in
the personal history of the hero's prosperity. The romance heroine
can, and will, subdue and refine the hero's sexual power; his economic power, however, is beyond her control to alter or purify. She
can only appropriate it, and, therefore, it must be pure from the
outset.

Since hard work is in its own right a valued male characteristic
adopted by the writers of romance, the hero puts long hours and
great amounts of energy into his work. But the dedicated business-
man turns out to be something of a problem. In the fantasy world of
marriage, the romance heroine will not spend her evenings at home
alone waiting for her tired-businessman husband to return. The
future promised the heroine is one of romantic love and high living.
Romance finds the solution to this dilemma in the businessman-
hero's decision to enter retirement or semiretirement. A favorite
motivation is overwork; fatigue conveniently strikes the robust hero.
Exhaustion is the good-faith evidence of real work and the pass-

3. Suzanne Simmons, *The Tempestuous Lovers* (New York: Dell, Candlelight Ecstasy Romance, 1981), p. 83.

port to a fantasy future for hero and heroine, a future of perpetual vacation:

"I have just come from three weeks of conferences and negotiations that would have sent most men straight into the hospital. I am still standing on my own two feet. . . . I plan to spend more and more time here [my beach house] and at a beautiful little villa in the south of France that I've just purchased. I am gradually turning over my business interests to others. By the time I'm forty I will be retired for all practical purposes. I mean to do a little lecturing, perhaps write a book, but that will be it. There's no sense in having money if you don't have the time to enjoy it."[4]

The hero's business skill and his virility are synonymous here: he is the rare man who can survive conferences and emerge unscathed from the rigors of negotiation.

When the romance writer finds her hero's occupation in the arts, many of the problems associated with the business world disappear; the romance hero as creative genius promises less nine-to-five awkwardness as well as more extravagant imagined pleasures. At the same time, the artist-hero, like the businessman-hero, is autonomous—always a "soloist," whether as novelist, painter, musician, or film director; he is never a member of a symphony orchestra or a repertory acting company. An obvious advantage of the artist-hero is that he needn't retire into marriage. In addition, romance presents artists as somewhat exotic, intrinsically romantic, and art as in itself seductive. The hero's art, as a result, can participate in the attempted seduction of the heroine. Sometimes this is crudely realized, as in the use of the heroine as a model for a painter. In other cases, the art form itself seduces; musicians offer serenades, and writers have language itself at their command.[5]

4. Ibid., p. 132.
5. Heroines with artistic ambitions of their own end up modeling for the artist-hero in Paula Edwards's *Bewitching Grace* (New York: Simon and Schuster, Silhouette Books, 1980) and Brooke Hastings's *Innocent Nights* (New York: Simon and Schuster, Silhouette Books, 1980). In Susanna Collins's *Flamenco Nights* (New York:

Shaun Sutherland, the hero of Lilian Peake's *The Little Impostor*, is a famous and financially successful novelist. Sutherland's novels have effectively seduced the heroine, Cara Hirst, before she ever meets him. One scene of lovemaking is initiated when Sutherland finds Cara rereading a passionate love scene in one of his books, a "chapter in Shaun's novel which, having read it so often in the past, she had learnt almost by heart." The part Sutherland's writing plays as proxy-seducer is made explicit at the close of the story when Cara tells him she has loved him from the moment they met: "Then she added more seriously, 'Even before I met you, I read your books, and I admired and respected you.'" The artist's life, moreover, can make room for the heroine. Once married to Shaun, Cara, trained as an historian, will become his researcher, or as he puts it, his *"alter ego,"* his "other self."[6] The heroine becomes the hero—or at least a useful and subordinated version of himself.

Occasionally, popular romance avoids the marketplace entirely in the interests of extravagant fantasy. In *A Girl Possessed*, Violet Winspear creates Pagan Pentrevah, scion of an uninterrupted line of Cornish barons. Throughout, Winspear plays on themes from Arthurian romance, enhancing the sense of an alien world, a medieval world of old romance into which the heroine has entered. The materials of such a story are highly provocative of fantasy, but they create their own problem by fashioning a hero who brings to mind the antipathetic qualities associated with the idle aristocracy. Winspear must demonstrate that Pagan Pentrevah, albeit a baron, has escaped the curse of leisure. At the very least romance must pay lipservice to the masculine and democratic values of work. In *A Girl Possessed*, it is no more than lip service: "For all that he was landed gentry Pagan Pentrevah was no idler, no eater of the lotus while others toiled. He often worked long hours on the home farm and

Jove Books, Second Chance at Love, 1981) the hero, a flamenco guitarist, woos the heroine with his music as well as with extravagant musical metaphors for erotic pleasure. Beckman's *Angry Lover* makes a good deal of the seductive power of the artist-hero's language (Patti Beckman, *Angry Lover* [New York: Simon and Schuster, Silhouette Romances, 1981]).

6. Lilian Peake, *The Little Impostor* (Toronto: Harlequin Books, 1977), pp. 47, 122, 188–89.

there were times when he took it into his head to go out with the trawlers who brought home their pilchards."[7]

Work serves as evidence for one aspect of masculinity, the ability to succeed in bourgeois society. With success, which is to say with money, comes the promised, if never articulated, ability to support the heroine in their future life together. But despite the emphasis on occupation, we do not see the heroes at work. What is shown is much more to the point, the evidence of successful work: possessions, cars and houses and clothes, yachts and servants, rich gifts and exotic vacations. All these objects signify power. To possess them is to be in a position of strength and security; to lack them, as the heroines of these stories do, is to be in a position of weakness and insecurity. Cara Hirst, employed as the nurse-companion of Shaun Sutherland's aunt, moves into "Wildsea," his castle-home, a world of ancestors and money. When the aunt piously points out that " 'it needs love . . . to make a house a home,' " Cara can only answer, " 'I wouldn't know. . . . I haven't got a home.' "[8]

The romance heroine may admire the hero's possessions, she may even be awed by them, but she never covets them. This constitutes a tricky problem for romance, since the heroine must not only be aware of the hero's display of consumer goods, she must see the hero at least in part *through* that display. There is no other concrete way to realize his economic power and communicate his economic allure. Nevertheless, her apprehension of the hero in terms of luxury consumer products can never even hint at any desire on her part for those products themselves. It is as if they were displays in a museum, artifacts beyond the possibility of ownership. Romance vigilantly protects the heroine's economic innocence; it is more precious than her chastity.

As a fetishist of consumerism, the romance hero is analogous to the man created by Hugh Hefner in *Playboy* magazine, but romance fiction presents a female version of a singularly male fantasy. Barbara Ehrenreich has analyzed the way in which *Playboy* recast the

7. Violet Winspear, *A Girl Possessed* (Toronto: Harlequin Books, 1981), pp. 136–37.

8. Peake, *The Little Impostor*, p. 112.

46

image of the American male from the monogamous, hard-working husband to the unmarried, hard-working consumer, showing the unattached man how to spend the money he made. As Ehrenreich puts it, the advertisements in *Playboy* present luxury items targeted for men, and "the new male-centered ensemble of commodities presented in *Playboy* meant that a man could display his status or simply flaunt his earnings without possessing either a house or a wife."[9]

From the point of view of female fantasy, the *Playboy* man is, curiously enough, nearly perfect. Like the romance hero, he is physically attractive, sexually alluring. And like the romance hero, he works hard and succeeds; moreover, he consumes, spending his money on material goods that mark him as a man of taste, sophistication, and chic. In fact, he has only one flaw: the *Playboy* man does not marry. As Ehrenreich explains, he remains single because he, and Hugh Hefner, know that women, whatever their talk of love, are really after men's money: "The issue was money: men made it; women wanted it." Women may pretend they want love, but in the terms of a 1953 issue of *Playboy* quoted by Ehrenreich, "All woman wants is security. And she's perfectly willing to crush man's adventurous, freedom-loving spirit to get it."[10] *Playboy*'s archenemy is the gold digger, and according to *Playboy*, all women are gold diggers.

Playboy conceives of the sexual-economic link as an opposition, in fact, an antagonism. Romance fiction acknowledges that construction but manipulates it in the service of the fantasy it weaves. Gold diggers there are, but the heroine is not among them. Nevertheless, the gold digger is a staple of romance; in the guise of the Other Woman, she becomes the principal defensive ploy in preserving the heroine's economic innocence. Not surprisingly, given the ways in which sexual and economic power are entangled in romance, the Other Woman—like *Playboy*'s gold digger—is both overtly seductive and economically self-interested. She aggressively uses her sexuality to try to win the rich hero. In the morality of romance, she betrays her womanliness. In the train of her mercenary motives, a series of

9. Barbara Ehrenreich, *The Hearts of Men: American Dreams and the Flight from Commitment* (Garden City, N.Y.: Anchor Press, 1983), p. 49.

10. Ibid., pp. 46–47.

other types of unwomanly behavior follow. The Other Woman may jilt the hero when he is poor and struggling. More sensationally, she may marry and then desert him, or commit adultery, even become pregnant with another man's child. Occasionally, pregnant with the hero's child, the Other Woman may entirely subvert womanhood by aborting the child.

The Other Woman represents all that the heroine is not, thereby highlighting the heroine's innocence, love, and true womanliness. Perhaps even more significantly, the Other Woman functions as a rationalization for the hero's behavior, his moods and bad temper, and his failure to believe in love. The hero was not born a *Playboy* man; the Other Woman made him one.

The romance hero is very often a man with a past, a dark history of involvement, suffering, and disillusionment at the hands of the Other Woman. The hero emerges with a generalized distrust of all women, believing them grasping, hypocritical, deceiving. The heroine, as a result, must demonstrate that she is different not only from other women in general but from the Other Woman in particular. Romance fiction always treats the hero's past history with a good deal more emotional respect than the heroine's. It is somehow taken as a given that heroines may have been orphaned, impoverished, jilted. But when these calamities occur to the valued and valuable hero they carry significant emotional weight.

Pagan Pentrevah has suffered greatly at the hands of the Other Woman. He tells the heroine in *A Girl Possessed* about his marriage to Roxanne, that he was "'besotted with her,'" and they "'loved in the heather and made our child there. . . . The child she didn't want and had taken away from her before it could be born.'" Roxanne's evil act, moreover, was not an isolated aberration of wickedness; added to it are an odd lot of associated sins: "'Her flirtations with friends of mine! Her glut of spending, and her quarrels with my staff! Her outrageous assumption that she was beauty and I was the beast who would condone the abortion of *my baby*!'" Hearing this story, the heroine feels "buffeted by a high wave that had taken away her breath and left her stranded and out of her depth."[11]

11. Winspear, *A Girl Possessed*, pp. 49–51, 67.

Even in these romances where no character explicitly enacts the role of the Other Woman, she still exists as a generalized conception, a model of male expectation against which the heroine must prove herself. In romance she is as pervasive as the gold digger in *Playboy*; it is the heroin̄ is unique. Thus, explicitly or implicitly, romance accepts the oy world of sexual warfare waged between hard-working, free ving men and cold-hearted women eager to barter sexuality rmanent economic security in the form of marriage. It is only uch an ideological position that the writers of romance can cre roes free to express themselves as moody, potentially violent satanic and at the same time invest them with such positive y and value. The heroine may not deserve such treatment, b hero has no way of knowing that he has encountered an an : female innocence and selflessness.

The *Playboy* man is an important analogue for the romance hero, as characterized by his financial success and array of possessions and by his defense of personal freedom, realized in romance as at least potential sexual promiscuity. But the hero of romance is a more serious figure than Hugh Hefner's beau idéal, more intense, more urgent, and much more serious in his sensuality. Sensuality, in the romance hero, is no mere expression of his freedom to enjoy himself, to play, for romance fiction locates in the sexuality of the hero the principal sign of economic power. To be sure, the connection between male sexual and male economic power in fiction goes at least as far back as Richardson; both Lord B. and Lovelace are aristocrats bent on having their sexual will of heroines who are their social inferiors. What differs in today's popular romance is that sexuality itself establishes the terms through which power is negotiated.[12]

The forged link between economic and sexual exploitation of women is now a commonplace of women's history,[13] and the specific

12. The sexual threat posed by men has existed side by side with that posed by the sexual woman, and specifically by her supposed insatiability. Romance has nothing whatever to say about the voracious sexual female; even the Other Woman is a much simpler, self-interested seductress.

13. See for example Ryan; Degler; Mary Poovey, *The Proper Lady and the Woman Writer: Ideology as Style in the Works of Mary Wollstonecraft, Mary Shelley, and Jane Austen* (Chicago: University of Chicago Press, 1984); Judith L. Newton, Mary P. Ryan,

dynamics of the relationship between the economic marketplace and the marriage market will be addressed in a later chapter. For our present purpose of understanding the romance hero it is important to see that the economic and sexual powerlessness of women, of the heroine, has been transmuted in fantasy into the economic and sexual potency of the hero, the object of desire. That strategy of romance fantasy, however, was not accomplished in a single step; it required a radical displacement in the literary representation of male dominance.

The example of Richardson reminds us that the novelistic tradition in England has a long history of associating the unrestrained expression of male sexual energy with evil. Lust is one important way of dramatizing the misuse of power. Nor are class distinctions absent from this view of male sexuality. Certainly, virginal heroines of gentle birth are never accosted, attacked, or "ruined" by lustful peasants or sex-crazed apprentices in English fiction. The heroine is threatened by superior power, both sexually and economically. But in this older tradition, as in the Gothic novel, the locus of dangerous male power is the villain. In the course of its development, the romance has taken that power, all that sexual and economic energy, and bestowed it on the hero.

As a form of romantic fiction, the contemporary romance is anomalous in its lack of a villain. All male potentialities, for good and for evil, have been incorporated into the single figure of the hero. The heroine, consequently, cannot elude male power; she cannot save herself from the villain and find refuge in a lover and husband innocent of male power. By adopting this strategy, the romance places its heroine in direct, if fantastic, relationship to the sources and the signs of male dominance.

The eradication of the villain and the concomitant metamorphosis of the hero has been a slow process. The first stages lay in a transfer of attributes between the two character types, a radical redistribu-

and Judith R. Walkowitz, "Editors' Introduction," *Sex and Class in Women's History* (London: Routledge and Kegan Paul, 1985); Joan Kelly, *Women, History, and Theory* (Chicago: University of Chicago Press, 1986); Julie A. Matthaei, *An Economic History of Women in America: Women's Work, the Sexual Division of Labor, and the Development of Capitalism* (New York: Schocken Books, 1982).

tion of the literary signs of the hero and the villain. The redistribution first occurred in Charlotte Brontë's *Jane Eyre*, and Brontë's legacy to romance requires examination.

The principal direct source of the contemporary romance hero, insofar as he manifests the threatening aspects of male power, is Brontë's Mr. Rochester. In his combination of qualities—his age and social superiority, his dark and threatening features, his unhappy experience with other women, and his violence of mood—Rochester is the ancestor of all contemporary romance heroes. Critics of romance have been quick to see Rochester behind the romance hero,[14] but have not examined the way in which romance fiction has adapted Brontë's dark hero to its particular uses. For contemporary romance, Rochester serves as a model for the possibility of redemption through the power of love, as the exemplar of the dark, sexual, threatening male creature who is tamed by innocence in the guise of a girl his inferior in age, experience, wealth, and station.

Here is Rochester as Jane Eyre first sees him, a stranger on a dark road:

> He had a dark face, with stern features and a heavy brow; his eyes and gathered eyebrows looked ireful and thwarted just now; he was past youth, but had not reached middle age; perhaps he might be thirty-five.[15]

14. In their guidelines for romance writers, Silhouette Books gives two examples for the hero type: "Heathcliff (WUTHERING HEIGHTS) is a rougher version; Darcy (PRIDE AND PREJUDICE) a more refined." Silhouette is on target with Darcy, but seems to have missed the boat with Heathcliff. Romance writers are hardly innocent in their exploitation of Brontë's hero. Violet Winspear has Pagan Pentrevah criticize the state of current fiction; rather than reading the Brontës, he laments, "'Girls are weaned on garbage-pail fiction.'" When the heroine asks, "'Am I supposed to regard you as Heathcliff?'", he replies, "'I prefer that it be Rochester'" (Winspear, *A Girl Possessed*, p. 44). For Rochester as a source for the romance hero, see, for example, Tania Modleski, *Loving with a Vengeance: Mass Produced Fantasies for Women* (Hamden, Conn.: Archon Books, 1982), p. 46. Elaine Showalter addresses the qualities in Rochester that appear in women's fiction, especially in a character type she calls the "brutes," "collateral descendants of Scott's dark heroes and of Byron's Corsair, but direct descendants of Edward Fairfax Rochester" (*A Literature of Their Own: British Women Novelists from Brontë to Lessing* [Princeton, N.J.: Princeton University Press, 1977), p. 139.

15. Charlotte Brontë, *Jane Eyre* (1847; New York: Random House, 1943), p. 83.

And as she scrutinizes him later by candlelight:

> I knew [him] with his broad and jetty eyebrows; his square
> forehead, made squarer by the horizontal sweep of his black
> hair. I recognized his decisive nose, more remarkable for char-
> acter than beauty; his full nostrils, denoting, I thought choler;
> his grim mouth, chin, and jaw—yes, all three were very grim,
> and no mistake.[16]

And here is a sampling of his contemporary avatars:

> His face had a darkly handsome stamp. . . . His nose was
> straight and chiselled, his jawline determined . . . [without]
> self-indulgent weakness. . . . his eyes became visible, their
> heavy lids drawn back. Green, mocking, they had dark pupils
> rayed with tiny threads of yellow that deepened their color.[17]

> The tanned, angular face with the hawklike nose still wore
> the mask of ruthlessness she remembered so well. There was
> nothing attractive about the hard set of his mouth and jaw, but
> there was that indefinable quality about him that reminded her
> of a sleek panther.[18]

> His cheekbones were high and chiseled with bold strokes above
> a wide squared jawline. The salient Roman nose balanced his
> features with an aggressiveness that heightened the devastat-
> ing power of crystalline green eyes. The parenthetical lines
> grooved on the sides of his mouth placed him in his mid-
> thirties, while his mouth, hard but with a certain curved sen-
> suality, hinted at cynical amusement.[19]

In adopting Brontë's dark hero, however, contemporary romance
fiction has stripped Rochester's physical attributes of their real import. It is essential to Brontë's story that Rochester *not* be handsome
because, for Jane Eyre, youthful male beauty carries a specific and

16. Brontë, *Jane Eyre*, p. 88.
17. Charlotte Lamb, *Retribution* (Toronto: Harlequin Books, 1981), pp. 26–27.
18. Yvonne Whittal, *Season of Shadows* (Toronto: Harlequin Romance, 1980),
pp. 14–15.
19. Edwards, *Bewitching Grace*, pp. 12–13.

potent meaning. Explaining her courage in standing and questioning Mr. Rochester, Jane accounts for it precisely on the grounds that he was not "a handsome, heroic-looking young gentleman." [20] A sudden meeting on a dark road with a gentleman both handsome and young would have dumbfounded Jane with a sense of her innate inferiority. The superiority of the handsome young gentleman was embedded in tradition—the tradition of social class and the tradition of romantic fiction. One tradition interprets the other: love bridges the classes. In other words, "a handsome, heroic-looking young gentleman" would establish not only his own identity, but Jane's as well, thrusting her into the sexual role created by class and romantic love. The awkwardness, the impossibility of such a role would have taken away Jane's courage.

Thus, though romance fiction picks up the salient features of Rochester, it transforms their purpose. Dark, angry-looking older men in contemporary romance do not relieve the heroine of the sexual role imposed on her by traditional fiction. To the contrary, such men, in defiance of Brontë, have now become the conventional objects of romantic love—and certainly of sexual attraction. As a result, today's heroines, perfectly at ease with handsome boys of twenty, quail before the descendants of Rochester.

Jane Eyre, of course, does meet a handsome young gentleman, in his looks a perfect storybook hero: "He was young—perhaps from twenty-eight to thirty—tall, slender; his face riveted the eye; it was like a Greek face, very pure in outline: quite a straight, classic nose; quite an Athenian mouth and chin. It is seldom, indeed, an English face comes so near the antique models as did his. . . . His eyes were large and blue, with brown lashes; his high forehead, colourless as ivory, was partially streaked over by careless locks of fair hair." [21] Although Jane goes on to undercut this description, to explain that "something about his nostril, his mouth, his brow . . . indicated elements within either restless, or hard, or eager," [22] St. John Rivers, if only for a moment, appears in the guise of the "handsome, heroic-

20. Brontë, *Jane Eyre*, p. 83.
21. Ibid., p. 260.
22. Ibid., p. 260.

53

looking young gentleman," which is to say, the traditional guise of the hero.

The fact that St. John looks the part of the hero is in itself striking. It is yet more significant that the qualities associated with him force comparison with Rochester's characteristics, establishing the paradoxical reversal of roles on which Brontë insists. Where Rochester is dark, St. John is fair. Rochester is nearing forty; St. John is not yet thirty. Rochester is sexually experienced; St. John virginal. Rochester is moody, passionate, capable of cruelty; St. John is emotionally controlled, incapable of violence. And whereas Jane must struggle to establish equality between herself and Rochester, she does not doubt that she is the equal of St. John Rivers.

Nevertheless, Jane confesses that she has feared St. John. The conventions of romance create Jane's anxiety, but once the buried assumptions are revealed, once the heroic-looking young man accepts his conventional role and proposes, Jane's fear passes away, she sees "his fallibilities," sees that "with that handsome form before me, I sat at the feet of a man, erring as I." St. John's power, significantly, is not sexual, a fact Brontë insists upon. On the contrary, his power, such as it is, lies in his apparent purity. But the beautiful man, denied potency, is vitiated, a hero manqué.

Certainly St. John is no hero for Jane; purity does not attract her. Like romance heroines of the present, she is drawn to the man with a past, and is deeply affected by the pain he has undergone at the hands of unscrupulous women. Jane learns about Rochester's past and sees the evidence of his suffering. "Pain, shame, ire— impatience, disgust, detestation—seemed momentarily to hold a quivering conflict in the large pupil dilating under his ebon eyebrow."[23]

Pure and handsome St. John elicits neither empathy nor ardor. When St. John proposes, Jane imagines her future with him, exposing her twin needs for passion and freedom to searching scrutiny. She envisages a marriage without passion as repugnant: "Can I receive from him the bridal ring, endure all the forms of love (which I doubt not he would scrupulously observe) and know that the spirit

23. Ibid., pp. 108 and 105.

54

was quite absent? Can I bear the consciousness that every endearment he bestows is a sacrifice made on principle?"[24] At the same time, Jane recognizes that passion is dangerous, that it threatens to constrain personal freedom, to shackle the individual to the desired object. For that reason, marriage to St. John might seem to promise a kind of safety, to guarantee a certain freedom: "I should suffer often, no doubt, attached to him only in this capacity: my body would be under rather a stringent yoke, but my heart and mind would be free. I should still have my unblighted self to turn to: my natural unenslaved feelings with which to communicate in moments of loneliness."

Nevertheless, Jane, who has sought liberty from the outset, rejects this marriage, learning that freedom of spirit thus achieved necessarily entails the annihilation of her passionate self: "but as his wife—at his side always, and always restrained, and always checked—forced to keep the fire of my nature continually low, to compel it to burn inwardly and never utter a cry, though the imprisoned flame consumed vital after vital—*this* would be unendurable."[25]

Insofar as she acknowledges her own potential for passion, Jane Eyre is like the heroine of modern romance, but the contemporary heroine altogether lacks Jane's integrity and self-understanding. Sexuality steals up on the modern heroine, disarming her, reducing her will to the point where she can no longer be held responsible for herself. Jane's character does not require this defense. Her intellect and her emotions inform her that freedom—or will—and passion are both necessary, both requisite to her fulfillment. Brontë needs no recourse to the favorite ploy of romance, the betrayal of the body that serves to justify female passion. But once the sexual self-awareness that marks Jane Eyre is denied the contemporary romance heroine, the romance hero, as we have seen, must necessarily bear, at least initially, all sexuality and all sexual power. The heroine becomes sexual only through his agency.

In her portrait of St. John Rivers, and in Jane's response—or lack of response—to him, Charlotte Brontë accomplished the complete

24. Ibid., p. 306.
25. Ibid., pp. 308–9.

55

dissociation of the traditional hero and sexual power. Certainly she had predecessors here, for the Gothic tradition had already well established the conventional lustful villain from whose clutches the hero would rescue the distressed heroine. But with Brontë, the heroine herself changes sides; Jane Eyre scorns the pure hero and desires the defiled and satanic Rochester. It is an astonishing modification, as if Samuel Lewis's Monk had ended up with the girl.

It is, at the same time, a difficult modification, costing Rochester a great deal.[26] Blind and maimed, feeble and doting, he is the physical manifestation of the hero conquered by love. Contemporary romance never goes so far; symbolic conquest suffices. But Rochester's metamorphosis is not entirely, perhaps not even most significantly, a change rooted in his character or even in the dynamic structures of *Jane Eyre*. In the person of St. John Rivers, Jane and

26. The blinding and maiming of Rochester have received considerable critical attention, generally in terms of Brontë's personal vision or in relation to conventions about women characters in the nineteenth century. Jean Kennard, for example, argues that Jane reaches maturity when she leaves St. John, but that the love story must end with marriage. The problem, however, is that Brontë "appears to recognize that the marriage of Jane to the old Rochester means submission to a master and is in conflict with her new found maturity." Jane's new financial independence "hardly solves the problem. So Charlotte Brontë maims him. . . . The relation of equals which Charlotte Brontë asks us to accept in the final pages of the novel is apparently only possible once Rochester is no longer fully a man" (*Victims of Convention* [Hamden, Conn.: Archon Books, 1978], pp. 91–92). Patricia Spacks, too, sees the wounding of Rochester as Brontë's way of making him Jane's equal, and she observes that this is "a disturbing resolution for the novel's clearly defined emotional issues." "Rochester, even crippled, remains the strong male on whom a woman can safely and happily depend, to whom she will willingly submit. But to deprive him of physical power helps to equalize the situation." Spacks, properly, finds "pathos" in such a resolution. "To fulfill Jane's need, it is necessary to handicap her lover." The maiming of Rochester becomes "an indirect expression of her anger [and] allows some parity to be achieved between men and women." In Rochester, "[a] man at once strong and weak," Spacks sees the "ideal realization of a female fantasy" (*The Female Imagination* [New York: Alfred A. Knopf, 1975], pp. 66–67).

Elaine Showalter also reads the maiming and blinding of Rochester, along with Jane's "destroying the dark passion of her own psyche," as the means by which the two become equals. But Showalter argues not for a female fantasy of the ideal man, but for a female fantasy of profound hostility: "The recurring motif in feminine fiction that does seem to show outright hostility, if not castration wishes, toward men, is the blinding, maiming, or blighting motif" (*A Literature of Their Own*, pp. 122, 150).

Brontë reject the traditional hero, and through the use of that character as a foil underline Rochester's kinship to the traditional villain. In making the villain, transmuted into the dark hero, the object of the heroine's desire, Brontë acknowledges passion as a motive for her heroine. But these are dangerous territories. Both passion itself and the passionate dark hero are perilous, eluding the control of the heroine. Only the metamorphosis of the dark hero into something less threatening can provide a resolution.

The usurping of the traditional hero's role by a character descended from the conventional villain is an essential feature of contemporary popular romance. Still, the question remains why the hero came to assume qualities traditionally associated with the villain. Why was it not possible, given the paradigm of power and sexuality in romance, to redefine the hero so as to associate passion and power with youthful, handsome, blond male characters? To a certain extent, the answer lies in the greater drama inherent in the struggle of the heroine against a figure conventionally associated with villainy. And in part it may be that the traditional figure of the hero had become too stereotyped as a defender of maidenly virtue to be reconceived as the emblem of threatening masculine sexuality.

More significantly, though, the power of the new villain-hero represents the power of men in general in a bourgeois and patriarchal society, a power most clearly perceived in terms of money and control over women's lives. Perhaps the most obvious aspect of this power in relation to women is its ambivalence. Conventionally, it is seen as holding out specific rewards for specifically female behavior. The ideology of male supremacy promises women love and protection, economic security earned without the need to enter the marketplace. This promise, however, conceals a concomitant threat, for if women have no need to *earn* economic security, they have every need to *deserve* it. Traditionally, women who have deserved protection under the sheltering wing of the patriarchy have been women whose modesty, submissiveness, and self-abnegation demonstrate their acquiescence to the status quo.

Of course, a crucial point about the status quo is that it remains a good deal less static than traditionalists would like to believe. During the late-eighteenth and early-nineteenth centuries, the gains made by the bourgeoisie created far-reaching changes in the distribution of power, principally affecting the position of the landed gentry in relation to men with new fortunes made in trade and manufacturing. This economic revolution created reciprocal changes in the romance, altering the figures of hero and villain as signs of the patriarchy. Once, the hero had been comfortably conceived as vested in land, power, and authority; consequently, he had no need of ambition, of the kind of energetic and even ruthless self-seeking popularly understood as necessary for success in the marketplace. Such negative attributes were associated with the villain, who imperiled not only the innocent heroine but in his very aggressiveness suggested a large-scale threat to the feudal aristocracy. As the sign of the negative aspects of the patriarchy, and particularly the bourgeois patriarchy, the villain's principal value for the fantasy world of romance lay precisely in the gratification his eventual destruction afforded.

Insofar as romance reflects real social conditions, it is always retrograde, supplying fantasy solutions to yesterday's dilemmas. For that reason, the Gothic romance, with its feudal distribution of power, rose and flourished just as the bourgeois hegemony was asserting itself. And in the same way, as we shall see, later Victorian popular romance, even in America, clung to an anachronistic economy of baronial estates and inherited titles. But such fantasy configurations could not last. Eventually, romance fiction had to take the bourgeois economic order into account, and it did so by according the hero some of the attributes believed to be essential for achieving success.

Women's fantasy, however, had no place for the ruthless captain of industry and no interest whatsoever in tracing the story of his economic rise. The best romance could do was adapt the new economic man to its own uses and fit him into its formulaic structures. To that end, the dynamic qualities of the villain, both his energy and his sexuality, were transferred to the hero. Not that the redistribution of attributes between hero and villain accomplished by Charlotte Brontë quickly took full effect on popular romance. But eventually Rochester cast a long shadow, for in the conception of the dark hero lay the strategies by which romance could respond to bourgeois society and at the same time express its own ambivalence toward patriarchal power in that world.

Furthermore, Rochester's legacy to the contemporary romance hero goes beyond the traditional attributes of the villain to include many of the qualities associated with the elemental figure of the patriarchy, the father himself. Rochester's age, the fact that he has already inherited his estate, his situation as a husband and, if not as a father, still as guardian to a ward, all contribute to his role as father. The hero of today's Harlequin romance has inherited these aspects of the father, increasing his ambiguity and further complicating the union of economic and sexual power. Brontë, unlike many contemporary romance writers, is very cautious here; she deliberately divorces age from sexual allure and divests her hero of all patriarchal signs, from his wife to his estate, before he and Jane marry.

For the contemporary romance hero, however, his superior age—like his considerable financial assets—unequivocally promises not only power but sexual allure specifically. Moreover, since such an age difference between lovers in no way reflects realistic, contemporary patterns of courtship and marriage, its value can only be symbolic; in his superior age, as in his superior social and economic station, the hero assumes the sign of the patriarchy and inherits, along with his other roles, that of the surrogate father.

To the extent that the hero assumes characteristics of the father, the romance heroine takes on the complementary role of child. We expect, of course, that the heroine will be virginal, that she will exist in the condition of girlhood as she awaits awakening into womanhood, but very often she is figured quite specifically in the condition of childhood, awaiting a kind of education into adulthood. Clement Vaulkhurst of Patti Beckman's *Angry Lover*, having confessed his love at the end of the story, justifies his earlier taunting and badgering of the heroine on specifically educational grounds.

> "I wanted to make you angry. . . . I goaded and taunted you because I wanted you to learn to stand up for yourself, to discover who you are and become an independent adult. I knew you could never be happy with me unless you could learn to live my kind of life, which meant living life on your own terms

and not worrying about what others thought of you. By keeping you furious at me much of the time, I think I succeeded in
bringing out the potential that has been stifled in you most of
your life." [27]

With the romance hero cast in the role of father or surrogate
father, the problem of hidden incestuous patterns necessarily arise.
It is not precisely a question of discovering incest lurking at the heart
of all popular romance, but much more a matter of sorting through
the confusion of male roles and male sources of power within the
single character of the hero. Nevertheless, there is no doubt that
some romance stories dwell with particular intensity on patterns of
relationships that flirt dangerously with kinship patterns, pointing
to incestuous motifs. Again, in *Angry Lover*, a great deal is made of
the fact that Vaulkhurst and the heroine are cousins. On the very
first page the heroine's mother asserts and immediately qualifies the
relationship: " 'Yes, we are second cousins, although it is not a blood
tie,' " and she repeats this three times within fifteen pages. When
Vaulkhurst meets the heroine and finally acknowledges that they are
" 'relatives—"kissing cousins," I think, is that awful, trite Southern
term,' " he at once transmutes the relationship, bringing it closer
to paternal, by making a point of the difference in their ages, a
difference that makes him " 'feel a bit more like an uncle.' " Given
such an insistence on kinship, it is not entirely surprising that the
hero concludes his avowal of love by remarking, " 'Since it started
by my finding you on my doorstep one night, I don't know if I
should adopt you or marry you.' " [28]

Some romance stories trespass further on the forbidden territory
of incest by setting up shadow love triangles. The hero is made to
believe the heroine's father is in fact a rival lover—both richer and
older than the hero. In Daphne Clair's *Never Count Tomorrow*, Lin
Blake is the daughter of a widowed Auckland magnate who denies
her nothing in the way of material goods, but fails to provide love.
Lin never admits to the hero, Soren Wingard, that her home, like

27. Patti Beckman, *Angry Lover* (New York: Simon and Schuster, Silhouette
Books, 1981), pp. 186–87.
28. Ibid., pp. 6, 19, 40, 46, 187.

the gifts she receives, comes from her father, and Soren's jealousy is fired. Convinced that Lin is living with a rich lover, Soren initiates a bizarre dialogue by challenging her: "'You're not in love with him,'" to which Lin equivocates, "'I'm very fond of him.'" Soren then refers scathingly to "the other man's" age: "'He is much older than you, isn't he?'"; "'Not elderly,'" Lin counters, "'Middle-aged, perhaps.'" Finally, Soren inquires, "'Is he married?'", and at last Lin becomes angry: "Did he really think she would live with a married man?" But she plays out the deception: "Coldly, she looked straight at him, and said, 'He has been married.'"[29] The coy and suggestive way in which this scene is played out invites an inference of incest. One is tempted to observe that living with a married man is precisely what all daughters do.

Incest patterns are somewhat muted in those romances where the hero's paternal function is more explicitly economic. Often such a plot involves real property, a specific patrimony. When the hero rescues the patrimony for the heroine, the patriarchy itself grows benign. For example, when her apparently wealthy father dies, one heroine finds he has left her penniless and in debt. A "run of bad luck" and some very bad "judgment on investments" have run up a mountain of debts. Even the family estate, her *home*, must be sold for the creditors. The hero eventually buys the old estate, and in marrying the heroine he at once restores the patrimony and returns her to the paternal home–which is to say, now the hero's home.[30]

Because the contemporary romance hero carries the residual character traits of three traditional male types—hero, villain, and father —he assumes various aspects of male power in patriarchal society and, therefore, takes on a complex set of functions in relation to the heroine. The hero's character traits are highlighted by the fact that he himself typically lacks a father; his condition as unfathered, or self-fathered man, enhances his autonomy. In the infrequent stories where the hero's father plays any role at all, he is usually a dim figure, sometimes long dead. In such cases the important point is

29. Daphne Clair, *Never Count Tomorrow* (Toronto: Harlequin Books, 1980), pp. 32, 160.

30. Tracy Adams, *The Moth and the Flame* (New York: Simon and Schuster, Silhouette Romances, 1981), p. 7.

frequently that this shadow-father had suffered sexual betrayal at the hands of the hero's mother. The real object of that betrayal, however, is not the father but the child; the wounded hero displaces his father as the victim of his own mother. Sexually unreliable, the absent father is also economically undependable, for he leaves the hero no patrimony. The hero, as a result, must become an entirely self-made man, economically and psychosexually.

The characters the modern romance conflates into the single figure of the hero necessarily produce ambiguities and contradictions. The villain, who lives on in romance through the hero's predatory sexuality, is at once feared and longed for. And the father, who moves, an unexorcised ghost, through romance, is at once tyrant and protector, an uneasy amalgam of the patriarchal power that both subjugates and supports the weaker woman. Power grows paradoxical, and appropriately so, for romance literature may have its particular strategies for subversion but not for the overt expression of the desire to overthrow the patriarchy. Ambivalence darkens the figure of the father as it has darkened the figure of the hero. But ambivalence is as far as romance goes, for it is the patriarchal aspect of the hero that shows itself capable of competing and succeeding in bourgeois society. Neither the heroine nor the blond and handsome traditional hero has that capability.

3

THE VICTORIAN POPULAR ROMANCE

I see the sagacious reader putting on his spectacles
to look for the moral. Good old soul!
With the help of a microscope he *may* find it;
may Heaven aid him in his search;
but lest he should fail, I must decamp.
Reader, adieu!

May Agnes Fleming, *The Actress' Daughter*

$\mathcal{W}$e have seen that Charlotte Brontë's Rochester, dark and brooding and masterful, usurped the role of romantic hero from the fair and handsome St. John Rivers and, in doing so, fathered a generation of contemporary romance heroes. But the ancestral line from Rochester to the sexually powerful heroes of Harlequin romances is not unbroken. As conventional, even banal, as the dark hero of contemporary romance has become, Brontë's reversal of traditional male character types was in her own time unsettling. Popular fiction writers were not ready to adopt and exploit that reassignment of masculine types and roles for nearly a century. As a result, the characteristics of Brontë's dark hero were returned to the villain in whom they had originated, particularly in the popular romance fiction of the 1860s and 1870s in America.

The period directly following the Civil War saw a burgeoning market for women writers of popular fiction. Story newspapers carried serialized novels for a growing audience of literate women with some leisure to fill with entertainment and some pennies to spend for sensational love stories. New publishing houses provided cheap books for this market, including reprints of novels serialized in the story weeklies. Like today's Harlequins, they served as outlets for industrious women writers. If few of them earned the success of an E.D.E.N. Southworth or a Fanny Fern, it was still possible for a number of women writers to earn a living, to support themselves by providing the fiction that fed both the story newspapers and the fantasies of their readers.

As in our own time, these years brought rising expectations for women engaged in or attendant to the struggle for women's rights, but also produced a reaction in women for whom the extension of privileges and rights seemed only to threaten whatever security they had managed to find within the patriarchal order. For such women, the principal if not the only escape from patriarchy lay in fantasy, and a whole industry was now dedicated to the production of romance fiction that promised just such an escape.

The parallels to our own time are striking, and the Victorian romances prefigure today's Harlequins, for both address the same dilemmas about power and powerlessness. But there are major differences as well, particularly in the fantasy solutions of the older romances. By foregrounding neither the hero nor the father but instead the villain, a figure in whom they found the most dynamic representation of the patriarchy, the writers of Victorian romances were able to dramatize more vividly the aggressive subtext of women's revenge and their appropriation of power.

The Victorian romance presents the villain in two plot configurations. In the more typical story, he stands in symbolic opposition to the hero; less frequently he metamorphoses into the hero. In either case it is always in the character of the villain, never the hero, that the writers of sensational Victorian romances invest all the evidence of masculine power, specifically its twin signs of sexual and economic energy.

Here, for example, is Rollyn Dane Conyers, the stock villain of a popular romance novel from the 1870s: "He was an English tourist, of a social grade superior to his compatriots on the *Bonivard*. He was . . . very handsome, with a dark and polished beauty seldom seen in Englishmen. His complexion was of an olive tint, his hair black as jet, his eyes of inky sombreness, yet with a red light gleaming in their depths."[1] Only the insistence that Conyers is handsome distinguishes him—with his dark face and gleaming eyes—from Jane Eyre's Rochester. Nothing at all distinguishes him from the hero of a Harlequin romance.

But Rollyn Dane Conyers is thoroughly a villain; no ambiguity marks his character. In the first chapter of this romance, *Beryl's Husband* by Harriet Lewis, Dane sees, meets, woos, and wins Beryl Star. Since we are dealing with a Victorian story for Victorian readers, wooing and winning mean marriage, but a secret marriage without the knowledge or approval of Beryl's guardian, which is as close to illicit sex as fiction of this period can come. Victorian readers knew they were not dealing with holy matrimony when the

1. Harriet Lewis, *Beryl's Husband* (1874; New York, Robert Bonner's Sons, 1891), p. 10.

villain said: "'But I will know her. . . . She is high-bred, of noble carriage, a trifle haughty and imperious, and is without doubt of noble birth. It is easy to see that she is romantic, impulsive and warm-hearted. I never before saw a woman whom I would be willing to marry, but I will marry her; I never set my heart on having anything but I possessed it. That girl will be my wife.'"[2]

To make doubly sure that conventional morality is piously upheld, the authorial voice intrudes to emphasize that Beryl is fated to suffer at the hands of Dane Conyers. The wedding, accomplished a few pages later, is called the "fateful ceremony," and Beryl is "so grave that one might have fancied that the pall of a sad future was shutting down already upon her young life." As the chapter closes, the heroine sets off "to walk to the end the thorny path whose beginning seemed so strewn with flowers."[3]

If this were the beginning of a Harlequin romance, one working with the early-marriage plot variant, Beryl and Dale would struggle against each other and against their own feelings for the other, eventually to understand and express their mutual love. In the meantime, there might be a good deal of sexual emotion; still, the resolution in love would preserve the heroine's chastity, keeping her a one-man woman.

That is not what happens in *Beryl's Husband*. Conyers tires of Beryl in a few weeks, and when he learns that she is not of noble birth, even (so we are led to believe) illegitimate, he abandons her, faking his own death and leaving evidence that the marriage ceremony was a sham. He returns to England, to the home of his uncle, the earl of Hawkshurst, who plans to choose as his heir one of his two nephews, Conyers and Noble Desmond. Obedience is the key to Hawkshurst's fortune; the estate will go to the nephew who marries Octavia, the apparent heir to the adjoining property.

To state the obvious, Noble Desmond is the hero of this romance. He and Beryl meet in London where, impoverished and alone, she struggles as an underpaid, live-out governess selling her embroidery to eke out a meager livelihood. Half-starved and exhausted, Beryl

2. Ibid., p. 11.
3. Ibid., pp. 20–21.

is nearly run over by a carriage, but Desmond rescues her. His credentials as a hero are as clear as Conyers's signs of villainy: "a slender, tall young gentleman, with white hands, a fair handsome face, and an air of well-bred languor and indolence."[4] "Languor" and "indolence" strike an odd note, even odder in light of the fact that Desmond has just leapt in front of a racing carriage. Moreover, he is not idle, preferring to return to his law studies in London rather than woo Octavia and win a fortune.

Languor and indolence may make no sense in terms of Desmond's actions so far in the story, but they are of considerable significance in leading us to a fuller understanding of the male roles assigned the hero and the villain. In *Beryl's Husband* the center of energy lies in the villain. In terms of the plot, he initiates the action and keeps it going—marrying and abandoning Beryl, discovering her later in London, alternately threatening her and asserting his love for her, and masterminding a plot to murder his uncle. In terms of the structural tension in the story, he embodies passion and sexuality. Although it is absolutely necessary that Beryl realize she never really loved Conyers, descriptions of him continue to emphasize his sexual power: "the darkly handsome face of Conyers, with that nameless charm and fascination about it."[5]

Noble Desmond, on the other hand, is quite devoid of vitality. After the rescue scene, his actions are few and usually futile. He does convince Beryl to marry him, and she, believing herself at once the victim of a false marriage ceremony and a widow, at last accepts him. But unlike the weeks of love following Beryl's first wedding, this marriage remains unconsummated. As Beryl and Desmond leave the church after their wedding, a carriage rolls past carrying Conyers and Octavia. With one look at her supposedly dead husband, Beryl swoons. That evening she slips away, once more impoverished and alone in London. So ineffectual is Desmond that he cannot locate her, allowing that success, too, to fall to the enterprising Conyers.

Besides trying to support herself by embroidering, Beryl is occu-

4. Ibid., p. 141.
5. Ibid., p. 236.

pied by her attempts to discover the secret of her parentage. What she finally learns, in the happy tradition of popular Victorian fiction, is that she is not illegitimate, that her mother died in childbirth, and that her father is—of course—Hawkshurst, conveniently without male issue. These facts elevate Beryl to riches and nobility, but heroic actions are necessary to demonstrate Beryl's personal, rather than merely legal, right to them. Therefore, in the final scenes of the novel, she disguises herself as an elderly widow and takes a position reading to the earl. He is now ailing, and, as Beryl discovers, the source of his illness is slow poisoning.

The story concludes when Beryl reveals the plot, foiling the villain and saving her father's life. What is critical here is that the heroine assumes the hero's conventional role; Desmond merely looks on. Moreover, the final scene emphasizes what the romance has developed from the outset, that the conflict exists between the heroine and the villain; the story is about them. The heroine has won everything, title and money, and won it in a struggle with the villain. Her marriage to the hero, moreover, brings *him* that title and inheritance, something he does not win by his own efforts but accepts at the hands of the victorious heroine.

The heroine has also won love, but this deserves some examination. She is already married; in fact, married twice, and bigamously because her marriage to Conyers, we learn, was not a sham. That marriage gave her the experience of passion, something we saw cool rapidly, at least for Conyers. But have we? Although Conyers's cooling ardor is made much of in the early part of the novel, later scenes insist on his undying love for Beryl. Wooing Octavia he feels "a fierce pang ren[d] his heart, as he wished in his soul that Beryl could have been well-born and an heiress." And at the very end of the story, drinking the poison intended for Hawkshurst, Conyers cries, " 'I drink to your healths, all of you. . . . My Lady Beryl, permit me to wish you happiness in your second marriage. I was not all bad; I have loved you from first to last; I love you still.' "[6]

Beryl's Husband closes, then, with the same confession of love we hear in contemporary romances; it is, of course, the villain, not the

6. Ibid., pp. 126, 344–45.

hero, who confesses, but it is in the villain that sexual energy lies and in whom sexual energy must be redeemed as love. Furthermore, love is called on to vitiate evil. Conyers, wife-betrayer and would-be murderer, cannot be "all bad" if he has loved Beryl "from first to last." But Conyers's confession of love does not initiate marriage and love forever after. His death follows instantly. Beryl lives happily ever after with Noble Desmond, who may not express passion but who has always believed in marriage. Well before he meets Beryl, Desmond has understood the seriousness of the marriage commitment "as something more than a union of hands and lands—as something that affects a man's entire destiny on this earth."[7]

No one could be tamer than the hero of such Victorian romances as *Beryl's Husband*. In part, this docility assures us that the heroine's future will be secure, not only in economic terms but in her relations with her legally all-powerful husband. The end of the story necessarily marks the end of the heroine's adventures; she must now settle into conventional wifehood. The same is true, to be sure, for contemporary romance heroines, but the modern heroine marries where she has triumphed, wedding the hero she has domesticated. Because the Victorian heroine wins her victory in a contest with another man, her future safety lies in the evidence of the hero's absence of threatening male qualities. The traditional distinction between hero and villain, reasserted in these stories after and in spite of Charlotte Brontë's example in *Jane Eyre*, necessitates the vitiation of the hero in the interest of allowing the heroine to triumph over male dominance, both sexual and economic, in terms even more dramatic than those afforded by the blinding and maiming of Rochester.

Harriet Lewis was a successful romance writer, her serials carried in the premier story weekly of the time, Robert Bonner's *New York Ledger*. Born in 1841, at fifteen she married Julius Warren Lewis, a successful writer under the name of Leon Lewis. The two of them wrote, independently and in collaboration, until Harriet's early death in 1878. The Lewises made a good deal of money from the serialization and subsequent book publication of their stories.

7. Ibid., p. 102.

Although they collaborated on much of their work, that collaboration took the form of Harriet's contributions to Leon's fiction; novels signed with Harriet's name were apparently entirely her own work.[8]

May Agnes Fleming, a contemporary of Harriet Lewis, was an even more successful writer of popular romance. Born May Agnes Earlie in St. John, New Brunswick, in 1840, she wrote a number of serialized novels for the *New York Mercury* and the *Boston Pilot* under the name Cousin May Carleton. She moved to New York sometime in the early 1860s, and in 1865 to Brooklyn, where she remained until her death in 1880. She married John Fleming, variously described as a machinist from St. John and a civil engineer from Brooklyn, with whom she had four children.

In 1868 she began to publish her stories with *Saturday Night*, another popular story weekly, earning a very respectable $50 for each installment, or between $800 and $1,000 for each novel. In 1871 she accepted a contract with the *New York Weekly*, which paid her $100 an installment for serial rights alone. In book form, her stories were republished by Carleton, who paid Fleming a 15 percent royalty. Additionally, advance sheets were sold to the *London Journal* for £12 pounds an installment. In short, May Agnes Fleming was a successful writer and a fairly rich woman. She wrote in as businesslike a way as she handled her contract negotiations. A thirty-week serial took her six weeks, working six days a week from nine in the morning until noon. The fruits of her industry: forty-three novels published—between 1861 and 1910.[9]

8. Albert Johannsen, *The House of Beadle and Adams and Its Dime and Nickel Novels* (Norman: University of Oklahoma Press, 1950), 2:183–86; Mary Noel, "The Heyday of the Popular Story Weekly," Ph.D. diss., Columbia University, 1952 (published as *Villains Galore* [New York: Macmillan, 1954]).

9. *New York Times*, 25 March 1880; Johannsen, *House of Beadle*, 1:112; Noel, "Heyday," pp. 391–94. Fleming's popularity is attested to in the number of publications and republications of her novels, a record that takes up eleven columns in the *Union Catalogue*. Her success, while considerable, in no way matches the extraordinary popular demand for E.D.E.N. Southworth, whose publication record consumes over thirty-two columns, and whose most successful novel, *Ishmael*, was reprinted at least nineteen times. Nevertheless, beginning in 1861 and continuing through the 1870s and, after Fleming's death, through the 1880s and until the depression of

The fiction published by Harriet Lewis and May Agnes Fleming represents a stratum of nineteenth-century literary production in America that has not received scholarly attention. Their work falls far outside the scope of conventional literary analysis; though feminists and specialists in popular culture have provided some studies of contemporary popular romance, this has not happened for its nineteenth-century counterpart. More genteel Victorian fiction in America has been ably treated by both Nina Baym and Mary Kelley, but Lewis and Fleming did not write genteel fiction. To adopt Mary Kelley's phrase, they were not "literary domestics."[10]

Both Baym and Kelley demonstrate that nineteenth-century women writers in America grappled with the dilemmas posed by women's enforced domesticity and their isolation from, yet subordination to, the public arena with its values of aggressive individualism and materialism. Set apart in a private space, in the home now reconceived as a privileged shelter from the turbulent marketplace, women nonetheless were pawns of the economic system. Marriage, for all the new celebration of conjugal felicity and romantic love, subordinated women to their husbands and, consequently, to the economic success or failure with which their husbands met. Baym and Kelley make clear the strategies by which the writers they study coped with the contradictions inherent in women's lives: essentially those strategies served to celebrate domesticity, albeit a domesticity happily, if somewhat uneasily, reconceived as the triumph of female virtue over the excessive individualism and aggressiveness of the marketplace.[11]

1893, publishers kept her books before the public. Scattered republication occurred until as late as 1910. Book publication of Harriet Lewis's fiction came after her death, chiefly in reprints by Roberts Bonners' Sons, beginning in 1883 and continuing until 1893.

10. Mary Kelley, *Private Woman, Public Stage: Literary Domesticity in Nineteenth Century America* (New York: Oxford University Press, 1985).

11. Nina Baym argues that in the novels she examines "domesticity is set forth as a value scheme for ordering all of life, in competition with the ethos of money and exploitation that is perceived to prevail in American society," for "in a world dominated by money and market considerations . . . [woman] was defined as chattel or sexual toy." Woman's fiction, therefore, is characterized by "stories in which, ultimately, male control and the money economy are simultaneously terminated."

Lewis and Fleming faced the same contradictions as other, better-known, nineteenth-century women writers. Growing up in the 1840s and 1850s, they entered a culture that had now fully consolidated the Victorian view of True Womanhood. Girls in the 1840s were socialized to emulate that model of female behavior; trained to the virtues of modesty, passivity, and subordination;[12] and educated to find in marriage and motherhood the fulfillment of their lives. The darker aspects of women's lives, powerlessness and isolation on the one hand, and the dangers of sexuality on the other, were not addressed save in the terms of a domestic ideology that disguised and even transformed them.

Like the "literary domestics," Lewis and Fleming wrote stories that provided women fictional solutions to real dilemmas. But unlike their genteel sisters, Lewis and Fleming rejected domesticity, with which they could reach no compromise. That rejection in itself represented an attack on patriarchal authority since, as Joan Kelly expresses it, "Patriarchy . . . is at home at home."[13] Rather than reform the patriarchal home as the domestic hearth, these two women

With this reversal of power relations, "the heroine uses her powers benevolently and rationally" (*Woman's Fiction: A Guide to Novels by and about Women, 1820–1870* [Ithaca, N.Y.: Cornell University Press, 1978], pp. 27, 40). Mary Kelley sees the "literary domestics" as accepting marriage as women's access to power: "When in the name of woman the literary domestics posed as moral and social critics of ambitious man and his materialistic society, they were calling into question male economic practices and pursuits upon which they themselves were dependent. It was men, not women, who were expected to be the money-brokers of society." Thus, "rather than claim title to property, the woman readily sought access to man's" through marriage. Nevertheless, "to be dependent upon man and his society was to be captive, and susceptible to man and the values of society" (*Private Woman, Public Stage*, p. 312).

12. Mary P. Ryan writes that though images of womanhood had been fluid early in the nineteenth century, "by mid-century, woman had been escorted to a definitive place in America culture." Even before the Civil War, books and games for little girls inculcated feminine values (*Womanhood in America: From Colonial Times to the Present*, 3d ed. [New York: Franklin Watts, 1983], pp. 113, 134–35). Carroll Smith-Rosenberg also comments on the socialization of women toward marriage and dependency and the concomitant "discontinuity between the child and adult female roles" (*Disorderly Conduct: Visions of Gender in Victorian America* [New York: Oxford University Press, 1986], p. 200).

13. Joan Kelly, *Women, History, and Theory* (Chicago: University of Chicago Press, 1986), p. 13.

chose a more dramatic escape from reality, formulating fantasies of absolute female autonomy, power, and property.

Sexual and economic issues are paramount, as the very titles of their romances make clear. Property, in the form of inherited estates, is frequently highlighted. Some inheritances remain in the male line, as in *The Heir of Charlton*; others, like *Sir Noel's Heir*, are more ambiguous; and some bequeath the property clearly to the heroine—*The Heiress of Egremont*, *The Heiress of Glen Gower*, *Edda's Birthright*. In some titles inheritance is buried, but implied, in a focus on ennobling marriages: *The Baronet's Bride* and *Guy Earlscourt's Wife*, where the hero's name itself suggests rank and property. Other titles point to sexual rather than property issues, specifically to charged and unsettling ambiguities in marital relationships: *Beryl's Husband* (where the heroine is bigamously remarried), *The Two Husbands*, *Neva's Three Lovers*. Some simply, and starkly, emphasize the dark prospects of marriage: *The Wife's Tragedy*, *The Fateful Abduction*, and *The Unseen Bridegroom* with its ominous subtitle, *Wed for a Week*.[14]

One May Agnes Fleming title most fully and simply expresses the fantasy ideal of both writers. *The Virgin Heiress*[15] promises property without marriage, economic power severed from sexual subordination, the absence of sexuality trumpeted in the triumphant "Virgin." In this title lie the theme and project of both writers.

Fleming and Lewis reject the cult of domesticity out of hand, and with it the cult of True Womanhood. Their rejection, however, does not take the form of revolutionary or even feminist polemics; like Harlequin romances, their novels embed an aggressive fantasy within a conservative frame. Like the Harlequins, they trace the

14. May Agnes Fleming, *The Heir of Charlton* (New York: G. W. Carleton, 1878); *Sir Noel's Heir* (printed with *Norine's Revenge*, New York: G. W. Carleton, 1875); *The Heiress of Glen Gower* (New York: G. Munro, 1892); *The Baronet's Bride* (Chicago: M. A. Donohue, 1868); *Guy Earlscourt's Wife* (New York: G. W. Carleton, 1873); *A Wife's Tragedy* (New York: G. W. Carleton, 1881); *The Fateful Abduction* (New York: G. W. Dillingham, 1907); *The Unseen Bridegroom* (New York: G. Munro, 1892). Harriet Lewis, *The Heiress of Egremont* (New York: Robert Bonner's Sons, 1889); *Edda's Birthright* (New York: Robert Bonner's Sons, 1890); *Beryl's Husband* (New York: Robert Bonner's Sons, 1891); *The Two Husbands* (New York: Robert Bonner's Sons, 1892); *Neva's Three Lovers* (New York: Robert Bonner's Sons, 1892).

15. May Agnes Fleming, *The Virgin Heiress* (New York: Street and Smith, 1888).

course of the heroine's life to the point of her marriage (sometimes to her reunion with a previously estranged husband) and leave her safely harbored in financially felicitous matrimony. But the formulaic narrative through which the happy ending is achieved has virtually no resemblance to contemporary romance. The story of the heroine's rise to success, the tale of her adventures, operates out of different strategies, and though authorial intrusions continually pay homage to conventional values, the story itself enacts a subversive and aggressive fantasy of appropriation and revenge. Both women directly, if fantastically, confront the complex fusion of sexual and economic power in men and the concomitant sexual and economic anxiety of women.

Of course, frank sexuality is no more a characteristic of Lewis's and Fleming's novels than of any other mid- and late-nineteenth-century fiction, especially fiction for women. Bourgeois ideology had succeeded by that time in reconceiving female sexuality and replacing the sexually voracious female with the asexual lady. Essentially, this new construction of female sexuality served the interests of men in bourgeois society,[16] but as Nancy Cott has shown, it had significant advantages for women as well, allowing them to be defined by "moral rather than sexual determinants."[17]

The problem, however, was that sexuality had gone underground,

16. Ryan sees the "social-psychological function of the chaste female [as providing] internal control of the economic lust and antisocial tendencies of the middle-class male." In the period of rapid industrialization, "private saving, be it of cash or semen" served economic ends (*Womanhood in America*, p. 221). Carl Degler, while warning that our accepting as "descriptive" those accounts of women's sexuality that were in fact "prescriptive or normative" has led to a "misreading of midcentury female sexuality," nevertheless notes that the conception of the sexual anesthesia of Victorian women played an important role in reducing family size and increasing family autonomy (*At Odds: Women and the Family in America from the Revolution to the Present* [New York: Oxford University Press, 1980], pp. 253, 258).

17. Nancy Cott argues that "passionlessness served women's larger interests by downplaying altogether their sexual characterization, which was the cause of their exclusion from significant 'human' (i.e., male) pursuits. The positive contributions of passionlessness was to replace that sexual/carnal characterization of women with a spiritual/moral one, allowing women to develop their human faculties and their self-esteem" ("Passionlessness: An Interpretation of Victorian Sexual Ideology," *Signs* 4 [Winter 1978]: 228, 233).

not disappeared, and its threat, unspoken, intensified. Genteel women's fiction responded as best it could, privileging the idea of marital love and reconceiving the hero as feminized, [18] his sexual menace at the very least subdued. Nevertheless, as Mary Kelley sees in the novels of the "literary domestics," sexual anxiety lurked beneath a discourse of love.

> In fact, as often as marital love bloomed in the fantasies of the literary domestics, fears of the dark shades of sexual passion in and out of marriage loomed in their consciousness. Talk had to be of love because the woman was destined for love, that is, she was destined to marry, but that made the woman dependent on love, subject to the whim of love, helpless before the fate of marriage. . . . But there was a disturbing thought that the linkage of love and marriage in the collective mind of young womanhood rendered women vulnerable to male sexual manipulation and exploitation.[19]

Lewis and Fleming maintain the conventional feminization of the hero, but pose an unconventional solution to the contradictions between love and sexuality: they confront male sexuality and defeat it. Coding illicit sexuality in the terms of a secret marriage, these authors frequently initiate their heroines, start them out on their adventures, specifically in terms of a sexual encounter. It is the villain who awakens, attracts, and abducts the heroine, and who soon deserts her. Thus, male sexuality is fully associated with evil male power and, in the person of the villain, it is driven out and eventually destroyed. An even more crucial point, however, is that the heroine experiences sexual attraction, learns firsthand its dangers, undergoes its penalties, and is as a result permanently innoculated against it.

The early sexual career of the Lewis and Fleming heroine not only armors her against sexuality in the future, it also makes an assertive counterargument to the double standard insofar as that is

18. Mary Kelley sees the hero of these novels as "exhibit[ing] the qualities of heroines" (*Private Woman, Public Stage*, p. 274).

19. Ibid., p. 260.

personified in the figure of the Fallen Woman. Through the device of the secret marriage, the heroine is made to trace the steps of the Fallen Woman. Her final triumph, consequently, subverts conventional morality, demonstrating—if never stating—that the heroine can fall and still entirely redeem herself. In fact, the fall is fortunate, for it serves as the necessary first step in her climb to success.

With the sexual menace out of the way, the heroines of these stories can set about their real business, the appropriation of economic power. Essential to this project are two narrative strategies: the splitting of the male figure into his three aspects of hero, villain, and father; and the escape into an anachronistic economy, locating economic power not in the contemporary marketplace but in feudal estates.

The fantasies of Lewis and Fleming could not be enacted against the entrepreneurial conditions of mid-nineteenth-century capitalism. The exclusion of women from that arena was more than even their fevered imaginations could deny. Moreover, the instability of the nineteenth-century economy posed a threat to women from which their enforced domesticity could not rescue them. As Mary Ryan has said, a wife's passive dependence on her husband's economic prospects made "the political economy of marriage" decidedly risky.[20]

The economic, like the sexual, solution offered by Lewis and Fleming substitutes aggression for denial. But the solution works only at the cost of economic anachronism. In place of the fluid and uncertain financial world of entrepreneurship their novels present the (presumably) stable world of hereditary lands and titles. In place of a market from which women are excluded stand inheritances that (again presumably) can be handed down in the female line. Obviously, the feudal economy both Lewis and Fleming create is as fantastic as it is anachronistic, but their very distance from this world makes economic wish-fulfillment possible, as it was not with the capitalist marketplace. At the same time, whatever fantasy gratifications the inheritance of feudal estates affords, the economics themselves still reflect—cannot finally allay—economic

20. Ryan, *Womanhood in America*, p. 138.

77

anxiety. The stable hereditary estates are always destabilized; inheritance is always in question and always threatened by the economic malice and entrepreneurial energy of the villain. Moreover, the resolution through inheritance in the female line, which is to say the very fact of the heroine's triumph, undermines the premises on which a feudal economy was based.

Harriet Lewis's and May Agnes Fleming's fantasies of women triumphant raise elemental questions of power, its relation to sexual energy, and the problem of women's acquisition of that power. In *Beryl's Husband*, as we have seen, Lewis locates power in the title and lands of Hawkshurst and then sets up an apparent competition between hero and villain for the inheritance. That competition is only apparent, however, for the hero disclaims any interest in the battle or its rewards. Like the heroine of contemporary romance, this hero is disinterested, morally above exerting any effort whatsoever in the interest of securing economic power. The heroic masculine role, then, is vacated until the heroine assumes it in order to join in the struggle and to divest the villain of all power, both economic and sexual.

As a defiance of patriarchy, *Beryl's Husband* is dramatically aggressive. Not only does the heroine take on and defeat the villain, acquiring the patriarchal inheritance, but a closer look at the relationships, real and implied, among the characters reveals what it is tempting to call a femininist version of the family romance. When Hawkshurst, the patriarch, summons Conyers and Desmond, sons of his dead brothers, to announce that one will become his heir, these cousins—hero and villain—become his symbolic sons, as well as each other's brother. As the earl's daughter, Beryl's symbolic relationship to both hero and villain becomes that of sister. The incestuous closeness of these ties is reinforced by the problem, pointed out in the title, as to which of them is Beryl's husband. In fact, just as they are each her brother, they are also each her husband. Although one marriage, to the villain, is consummated sexually, and the other, to the hero, is not, both marriages have the same effect on Beryl's life. As the structure of the plot reveals, marriage plunges Beryl into isolation and poverty. The simple rhythm of the plot is one of marriage (to

Conyers), followed by a period of isolation and poverty in London, then marriage (to Desmond), followed by a period of isolation and poverty in London. After that comes Beryl's triumph, the discovery of her true birth and her rescue of her father from the hands of her brother/husband.

It would be hard for a fictional structure to make it clearer than this that marriage is no answer to a woman's need for security. In the interest of real security Beryl must wrest power from the hands of male authority. The kinship relationships in *Beryl's Husband*, moreover, displace the power struggle from the adult world to the world of childhood, the world of fathers and brothers; in this desperately overinvested fantasy, the daughter proves her courage and heroism by besting the bad brother and demonstrates her love by rescuing her father from imminent murder at that brother's hands.

Harriet Lewis's *Her Double Life*, serialized in the *New York Ledger* in 1869, recapitulates the patterns of *Beryl's Husband*. Lord Trevelyan plays Hawkshurst's role; unmarried, he must bestow his lands and title on one of two nephews, the noble Geoffrey or the evil Adlowe, who has convinced his uncle that Geoffrey tried to murder him for the inheritance. The heroine, Giralda, is Geoffrey's daughter and the patriarch's granddaughter, and the story—despite its extraordinary complications—falls, like *Beryl's Husband*, into a simple pattern of repetitions. Giralda, a stranger to Trevelyan, takes a position as reader-companion to him, and he soon decides to adopt her, first as his granddaughter and later as his niece. When Adlowe learns that Giralda has become Trevelyan's heir, he determines to marry her although he had, up to this point, pursued her mother. As the generational distinctions collapse, the story progresses through a pattern of flight, capture, and rescue, repeated three times. Giralda flees only to be captured by Adlowe, and though twice rescued by the younger secondary hero, Paul Grosvenor, his relative ineffectualness is underlined by Adlowe's continued success in recapturing her.

In *Her Double Life*, as in *Beryl's Husband*, hero, villain, and heroine become symbolic siblings: Geoffrey and Adlowe as blood relatives, cousins/nephews; and Giralda as daughter to one, cousin to the other, and adopted granddaughter/niece to Lord Trevelyan. Giralda, like Beryl, brings the story to the point at which the villain's schemes and plots can be unmasked and the hero reinstated.

As a villain, Adlowe has all the characteristics we saw in Conyers, and all intensified. He is even more exotic and more dangerous in appearance, with eyes "cruel in expression," and "shaped like the eyes of a Chinaman." Or "gleam[ing] from cavernous sockets, and . . . encircled with purple rings." Or "red, dark-circled," marked with a "burning glare." Driven by lust and greed, he is given to speeches about breaking the heroine's will or spirit. Having captured Giralda, he tells her he will keep her in a secluded house until " 'your spirit is broken sufficiently to make you submit to my will.' " The sexually threatening villain is challenged, in brave words, by the young hero: " 'Your persecutions of the innocent and helpless will soon cease. I am the champion of these wronged people.' " [21] But his heroic boasts are no more effective than the threats of the villain. The male characters deal in words, but the heroine acts and prevails; she is her own champion.

The novels of May Agnes Fleming share the principal structural elements seen in Harriet Lewis's fiction: the triangle of hero, heroine, and villain; the resolution of that triangle into a conflict between the heroine and the villain; and the final victory of the heroine over the person and the property of the villain. There are, however, two important differences between the novels of Fleming and Lewis. Fleming typically gives her heroines more overtly assertive, even rebellious, personalities, especially as children or young girls. And Fleming's treatment of male characters is often more ambiguous than Lewis's, for while Fleming sometimes opposes a villain to a hero, she is just as likely to conflate the two into a single figure. The combined hero-villain provokes some comparison with contemporary romance, although, as we shall see, the dynamics of reformation are somewhat different.

When Fleming does separate hero and villain, creating opposing male characters, the similarities to Lewis's stories are very strong,

21. Harriet Lewis, *Her Double Life* (New York: Robert Bonner's Sons, 1883 [first serialized in the *New York Ledger*, 1869]), pp. 12, 478, 484, 418, 322.

indicating how pervasive a formula existed for this kind of romance fiction. In *Norine's Revenge*,[22] published in book form in 1875, the heroine becomes engaged to steady, honorable Richard Gilbert, a respected lawyer, old enough to be her father, and entirely devoid of sexual energy. Norine becomes infatuated, however, with the villain Thorndyke, agreeing to meet him secretly on the eve of her wedding. Thorndyke abducts her and they are secretly married, the abduction serving to mitigate somewhat Norine's responsibility and guilt for the sexually charged convention of the secret marriage. Thorndyke has the full complement of a villain's characteristics; he is young, idle, sexually fascinating, and he anticipates coming into a fortune when his rich guardian dies.

Thorndyke, of course, tires of Norine and soon abandons her. When her passionate love turns to despair, Norine vows revenge. Eventually she ends up as a companion to Thorndyke's guardian, and once they have come to know and like one another, she tells him her story. He adopts her and, having arranged for her to inherit all his money, conveniently dies. In possession of Thorndyke's money, Norine now takes possession of his heart, for when he meets her again, some years later, she has matured into a poised and beautiful woman. Like Conyers in *Beryl's Husband*—and like the hero of contemporary romance—Thorndyke suddenly experiences and acknowledges his love for Norine. Her vengeance is complete when Thorndyke's wife, at Norine's instigation, overhears his confession of love for Norine and when the two women, bonded in a kind of furious sisterhood, triumph over him. Norine then assumes responsibility for Thorndyke's wife and children, thereby taking away his only remaining male prerogative, while Thorndyke goes to seed in the Bowery, eventually committing suicide. As an afterthought, Fleming has Norine and Richard Gilbert marry.

As *Norine's Revenge* demonstrates, Fleming has no difficulty with the formula of woman's triumph over the villain and her acquisition of all the signs of his male power as a deliberately determined act of revenge. But in those stories with a single male character, at once hero and villain, a somewhat different dynamic is played out. Be-

22. May Agnes Fleming, *Norine's Revenge* (New York: G. W. Carleton, 1875).

cause of Fleming's increasingly patent scorn for men, the complete transformation and redemption of the villain become exceedingly problematic. Deprived of the pleasure of killing him off, she adopts the strategy of ignoring him. Fleming typically creates a menacing villain and thoroughly exploits his possibilities as an antagonist to the heroine, but when the time comes for his change of heart, she loses interest. Tactics aside, Fleming's essential attitude toward male figures remains the same: villains are dreadful but interesting; heroes are dull stuff.

But Fleming's deepest interest, like Lewis's, lies in the heroine, a characteristic that distinguishes their work from contemporary romance, where narrative focus is typically fixed on the heroine but where value and intensity are invested in the hero. Fleming's heroines, again like Lewis's, fall victim to the villain through some early error of judgment. Once betrayed, their female innocence and vulnerability give way to purposeful, assertive behavior.

It took Fleming some time before she could overcome, at least in her fiction, the powerful effects of female socialization. In her first novels she does not present heroines characterized by unfeminine assertiveness and self-esteem. Concomitantly, she does not problematize the class status of her heroines, placing in them in the positions of (supposed) orphans or foundlings for whom some degree of assertiveness would be necessary for social elevation. In her earliest work, she is satisfied to rest her heroine's significance on traditional formulaic characteristics of beauty and social position. In her first published book, *Sybil Campbell; or, The Queen of the Isle* (1861), Sibyl,[23] the titular heroine, is a beautiful aristocrat, complemented by the character of young Christie, a child of sixteen with no family, no history, not even a last name. Although Willard Drummond, the hero-villain, loves Sibyl, he secretly marries Christie. The machinations of a very complex plot bring about Christie's apparent death; knocked unconscious, she is carried away by the tide. Subsequently, Sibyl is accused of the murder, tried and found guilty, condemned to death.

23. Although the name is spelled "Sybil" in the Union Catalogue listing of the title of Fleming's novel, it is spelled "Sibyl" throughout the text.

The resolution of *Sybil Campbell* finds Christie, near death from consumption, braving a frightful storm to save Sibyl from execution. Cristie's death scene follows closely on the rescue, and in her dying moments she pleads with Sibyl to forgive Willard for his secret marriage and to become his wife. It is Christie who confesses, speaking for the now reconstituted Willard, the hero's love for the heroine. " 'Sibyl, I am dying! You will not refuse my last request? Oh, Sibyl, in a moment of thoughtless passion he married me; but all the time he loved you best. I can see it all now. He loved you then—he loves you now, better than all the world.' "[24] Christie then conveniently dies; Sibyl and Willard marry.

In this early work, Fleming awkwardly splits the character of her heroine. Sibyl, presumably because of her superior station, is rewarded with the hero; Christie, conversely, is entirely victimized. Christie's faults are no more than her apparent illegitimacy and consequent obscurity and lack of cultivation, faults romance writers, including Fleming, knew how to dispense with handily. But Christie must lose, for she is pitted against superior wealth and power, in the hands not of a man but of a woman. In this early work, Fleming cannot discover a better way to express female power than in its innate superiority of beauty and station, on the one hand, or in the moral pathos of sacrifice on the other.

As Fleming discovers how to shape the materials of romance to her particular ends, she learns to subordinate class interests in favor of gender interests alone, to present a poor and unconnected girl and carry her to victory and dominance through a conflict established squarely along lines of gender. Once this occurs, the conflict in Fleming's fictions necessarily turns from what had been a single focus on the dangers of passion to a much more expressive fusion of sexual and economic energy. Thus, in her later novels she comes to deal ever more directly with the issues of women and power. At the same time, and perhaps as a result of her obsession with power, Fleming treats marriage, and even love, with growing distrust and contempt. To be sure, she pays lip service to the conventions in

24. Fleming, *Sybil Campbell; or, The Queen of the Isle* (New York: Street and Smith, 1885), p. 388.

pious authorial asides, but the charged fantasy presented in the fictions tells quite another story.

The orphaned girl, without family or name, becomes Fleming's favorite heroine. Obviously, such a figure allows for pathos, drama, and the propitious late discovery of a wealthy, noble father. At the same time, orphanhood enhances the heroic qualities of the heroine; like the hero of contemporary romance, she is unfathered—and unmothered—and must make her way alone. Finally, orphanhood has a special value for Fleming. Girls without parents, and especially without mothers, lack a proper upbringing; as a result, the unfeminine assertiveness and ambition that Fleming so much admired find an alibi in inadequate nurture.[25]

In *The Actress' Daughter*, Fleming matches her ambitious orphaned heroine against a male character who is both hero and villain. Georgia Darrell is the daughter of a woman who was disowned after running off with an actor. Abandoned and destitute, she dies, and the infant Georgia is brought up by a rural spinster. As a girl, Georgia embodies the characteristics Fleming most admires—independence, daring, spirit. Even as a baby she has "great, wild, glittering black eyes, long tangled masses of coal-black hair . . . a strange, unique face for a child, full of slumbering power, pride, passion, strength, and invincible daring." Still a child, she meets Richmond Wildair, the villain-hero. His physical description leaves no question of his essential character: "not exactly a handsome face, yet it was full of power—with keen, intense, piercing eyes."[26]

Even as a child Georgia becomes engaged in a struggle of wills with Wildair. At the outset, Wildair's will is the stronger, and Fleming's language suggests that his superior strength of will lies precisely in the power of his male sexuality: "the hitherto unconquered Georgia felt that she stood in the presence of a strong will,

25. To be sure, the orphaned heroine was hardly unique to Fleming, nor was the strategy of excusing errors of judgment and behavior on the grounds of a girl's motherlessness. Isabel Archer, to name one example, suffers from the same problem. The difference in Fleming is one of degree; she allows her heroines extravagant displays of ambition and aggression.

26. Fleming, *The Actress' Daughter* (New York: G. W. Carleton, 1886), pp. 24, 54, 74.

that *surmounted* and *overtopped* her own by its very depth, intensity and calmness" (emphases mine).[27] The struggle intensifies as Georgia grows into adolescence and, without benefit of an appropriate female mentor, becomes increasingly bold. Without question, Fleming admires Georgia's spirit and freedom, but convention demanded that these qualities eventually give way to more modest and womanly characteristics. Thus, the story line celebrates spirit, while authorial intrusions make conventional—and often halfhearted—amends. Describing her child-heroine as "generous, frank, and truthful," yet "proud, passionate, sullen, obstinate, and vindictive," Fleming mitigates these faults by ascribing them to a failed upbringing: "not a vice that child possessed that a careful hand could not have changed into a real virtue, for in her sinning there was nothing mean and underhand."[28]

In Georgia's relationship with Wildair, however, her spirited character becomes something he yearns to tame into obedience, not educate into virtue. In the early scenes between them, Georgia is frequently figured in animal imagery, but the imagery stresses freedom and power, not bestiality. Thus, Richmond sees "a fierce flash of [her] eyes [that] reminded him of a panther he once shot." Even as Georgia reaches adolescence and is capable of exercising greater control over herself, it is no more than "the calm that precedes the tempest, the dangerous spirit of the drowsy and beautiful leopard." The effect on Wildair is to goad him into an even more exacerbated will to dominance: "'I shall conquer her more thoroughly yet before I have done with her. I expect she will struggle against it to the last gasp, but she shall obey me.'"[29]

Georgia's personal ambitions are distinctly unfeminine. She plans to pursue male goals—money, power, adventure. "'I intend to be rich,'" she tells a friend; "'it's riches moves the world. . . . Poverty is the greatest social crime in the world.'" This female child knows that "'wealth brings power,'" and that such power cannot be gained through marriage. One day, after she has become rich, she will

27. Ibid., p. 74.
28. Ibid., pp. 77–78.
29. Ibid., pp. 80–81, 116, 99.

"'settle down and marry a prince,'" for illegitimate foundling that she is, Georgia asserts, "'I am good enough for any prince or emperor that ever wore a crown.'" And later she taunts Wildair by vowing that "'I shall go and seek my fortune. . . . [I shall] found a colony, find a continent, make war on Canada, run for President, teach a school, set fire to Cuba, learn dress-making, or set up a managerie [sic].'"[30] But when Georgia's trials begin, they do not come as a result of her unfeminine ambitions. Fleming will not punish her for adopting masculine goals; she has no quarrel with Georgia on these grounds, authorial rhetoric to the contrary. Georgia's mistake comes in marrying Richmond Wildair.

Wildair is very rich, his family the local aristocracy. But despite the great social distance between him and Georgia, he proposes and she accepts. Fleming, always dubious about the benefits of matrimony, is particularly pessimistic in this case. Even Georgia is uncertain, half-joking about marriage "'enslaving her,'" and seeing herself, in her wedding clothes, as "'arrayed for the sacrifice.'" Fleming makes no jokes: "Georgia Darrell is no more; the free, wild, unfettered Georgia Darrell has passed away forever, and Georgia Wildair is unfettered no longer; she has a master, for she has just vowed to obey Richmond Wildair until 'death doth them part.'"[31]

Richmond immediately sets about remaking Georgia, determining to turn his wife into a polished society woman who "*must* lose this country girl awkwardness . . . and do the honors of my house as becomes one whom I have seen fit to raise to the position of my wife.'"[32] Scorned and tormented by Wildair's family and friends, Georgia soon regrets her marriage; her feeling of suffocation increases and she speaks out rebelliously. Wildair grows more cruel and supercilious, his language more openly and intensely villainous. Finally, driven desperate by the taunts of a female cousin, Georgia attacks her physically, crying out that she will no longer be Wildair's slave.

30. Ibid., pp. 125–27, 147.
31. Ibid., pp. 177, 179, 181.
32. Ibid., p. 189.

The marriage scenes in *The Actress' Daughter* are horrific, filled with violence. In part this is necessitated by the plot, providing adequate motivation for Georgia to run away, but in part it seems to express genuine feeling on Fleming's part. Marriage, it appears, even a marriage that seems based on mutual love, is a perilous undertaking for a woman. Equality in marriage does not come automatically.

Georgia runs off to New York and faces the problem of supporting herself. She finds a position as a governess, and the loss of her freedom brings her close to madness. The passing days bring numbness, with only occasional rebellion "against the intolerable servitude." After six months, she is filled with "a lassitude, a languor, a dull, spiritless gloom," and Fleming comments that "it was possible a year or two, of such existence, would have found her in a lunatic asylum or in her grave."[33] Eventually, however, it would appear that Georgia's suffering is at an end. She learns that Wildair now knows his mother caused all his marital difficulty, that he continues to adore his wife, that he is searching everywhere for her. But Georgia does not reveal herself, nor does she return to her repentant and loving husband: "Somehow, she scarcely could tell why, she did not wish to meet [Richmond] yet; if ever she returned to him, it must be in a way different from what she had left. . . . she had a vehement desire to win wealth and fame, and return to Richmond Wildair as his equal in every way."[34]

Still freed, at least for the time being, from the role of wife, Georgia can now fulfill the ambitions she had for herself from the outset. Moreover, having learned that marriage is an unequal contest for dominance, with enslavement for the weaker, she recreates herself as Wildair's equal.

When Georgia returns to New York it is not as the typical romance heroine of the period, faced with the need to find humble work to support herself. Having taken up drawing and then painting while a governess, and having saved six months' wages, she goes to New York to make her fame as an artist. She submits her painting

33. Ibid., pp. 280, 299.
34. Ibid., p. 318.

of *Hagar in the Wilderness* to a competition, and she wins. When the identity of the artist is revealed, the response is sexist incredulity: "they fairly laughed at the notion at first"; " 'A lady paint that!' "; " 'I never heard of such a thing.' "[35]

Now successful in her own right, indeed famous, Fleming's heroine is ready—not to return to Wildair—but to become rich! Reunited with a long-lost brother, Georgia learns they both have inherited a fortune from their grandfather. Like Georgia, her brother knows what is at stake: " '[My] sister shall never go back penniless to her husband. . . . he shall find her his equal in wealth, as in everything else.' "[36] But it is still not time to return to Wildair, not time yet to decline into wifehood. Georgia and her brother tour Europe for a year.

At last Fleming must bring her story to a close by reuniting the married pair. It is necessary to summon the long-absent Wildair: "And where, meanwhile, was he whose willful blindness and haughty pride had brought on his own desolation?" It is not Georgia who is seen as suffering, for indeed she is not; the hero-villain has caused himself considerably more pain, we are told, than he brought the heroine. And quite right, says Fleming, "these tortures of doubt, and uncertainty, and hope, and despair, served Richmond just exactly right."[37] But the hero's suffering cannot have interfered with his career; he is, after all, the heroine's husband. Therefore, Wildair is the newly elected governor of New York.

When resolution and reunion come, Fleming loses interest. The man and woman she reunites are strangers to us, for Victorian convention now requires a noble husband and a gentle wife. Wildair's nobility is carried in metaphors of royalty, his "kingly form," his "princely brow," and in his appearance before his constituents looking down on them "as a king might on his subjects." As for Georgia, "the old flashing light had left her eyes, and in its place was a sweetness, subdued, gentle, and far more lovely. . . . far more sweet, tender, and lovable . . . than the haughty, fiery, passionate Georgia."

35. Ibid., p. 332.
36. Ibid., p. 347.
37. Ibid., pp. 352–53.

This change is attributed to religion, which has newly created this "humble, gentle, loving girl, meek in her great forgiveness."[38]

Although neither character change is convincing, or at all interesting, Wildair's is the more improbable, for he has virtually disappeared from the story for nearly two hundred pages. This is transformation from necessity, the necessity dictated by conventions of fiction and society. Making allowances for the genteel conventions of Victorian fiction, we can see that Wildair is closely akin to the modern romance hero in the progressive stages through which he passes: attraction to the heroine, sexual and psychological dominance over her, and final acquiescence to the power of his love for her. At the moment of acquiescence, as in contemporary romance, the hero emerges from behind the mask of the villain. But Wildair is less than satisfying in the role of redeemed man. For one thing, Georgia and the reader have known him from his youth; his life story is open to us and we know that no unhappiness, no betrayals, have caused his misogyny. Moreover, he has known Georgia from her childhood and can have no misapprehensions about her. His cruelty and violence are not even minimally motivated as they are in the contemporary hero; Wildair simply *needs* to destroy Georgia's spirit and autonomy. Most important, unlike today's romance hero, Wildair is not valued by the author. Fleming does not even like him enough to keep him in the story once it is possible to dismiss him. The fact that we do not follow Wildair, do not see him arrive at the recognition of love, demonstrates the degree to which Fleming fails to find him interesting in the role of hero. As a villain in charged conflict with the heroine, he engages her; later, like the heroes in stories where a separate villain appears, he is dull and ineffectual, kingly metaphors notwithstanding.

Villains, however, are interesting because they are the locus of power and because, as such, they call forth the energies of the heroine in combat over that power. Villains are the only male characters in whom Fleming and Lewis invest any narrative intensity whatever. Like the contemporary hero, they have a powerful glamour, even if it is almost entirely a negative glamour. The heroine's interaction

38. Ibid., pp. 366, 363, 482–83.

with the villain, moreover, is of great interest and importance in these stories, unlike her interaction with the hero, which leads only to the safe and uninspiring harbor of marriage. Locked in combat with the villain, the heroine can struggle for what is important—for power. Marriage, as *The Actress' Daughter* makes plain, is not the road to power.

As we have seen, Lewis and Fleming recognize the powerlessness of women within America's competitive market economy and displace that economy with an anachronistic fantasy of the inheritance of great estates and vast fortunes. But in their romances, the fantasy of inherited property is itself powerless to affect the way in which money and evil are deeply implicated in each other. Inheriting money, like earning money, requires energy in these stories, for where inheritances are always disputed, one potential heir must struggle to win out over the other. In the stories of Fleming and Lewis, it is always the villain who puts up the struggle. Harriet Lewis, especially, makes it patent and significant that the energy the villain expends in pursuing money is energy spent in plots, schemes, and acts of violence—energy expended in the interest of evil. Thus, although the real marketplace is displaced in fantasy to the world of fabulous inheritances, these stories continue to reflect women's apprehension of and hostility toward the marketplace and the money ethos dominating America.

The drive for money and property, like the sexual pursuit of the heroine, is both marked as evil and charged with vitality. Sexual and economic rapaciousness are twin expressions of male energy, in fact the only expressions of that energy Fleming and Lewis could contrive, for in economic and sexual desire are constituted the figure of man as the enemy. The villain, in expressing the paired energies of male dominance, leaves no role for the hero to fill; he is divested, from the outset, of any source of energy or of power.[39]

39. In some stories, and Fleming particularly liked this pattern, the hero is forced into exile and must redeem himself, must make his own way before the heroine restores him to his fortune. In such stories he almost inevitably becomes well known and well-to-do as a writer. This pattern enforces the effeminacy of the hero, drawn into a profession dominated not only by women in general, but in this case by Fleming in particular. Examples include *Who Wins?*, *Guy Earlscourt's Wife*, *The Heir of*

The hero is defended from the evils associated with money getting, but that very protection debilitates and emasculates him. Nor do Fleming and Lewis find that the vitiated hero presents any problem in their fictions, because marriage and romantic love are never the real issues in their stories. These Victorian romances, for all the traditional pieties maintained in authorial comments and in the conventional concluding wedding or reunion, are much more naked statements about power than are today's Harlequin romances.

What Lewis and Fleming sacrifice, that is, by contemporary standards, is any fantasy gratification in terms of romantic or sexual love. Sexuality is not their heroines' goal, not an end but merely a stage, something to be overcome. Illicit sexual union, encoded as a secret marriage, proves again and again to be the most powerful agency for simultaneously subverting and empowering the heroine. It is the passionate liaison itself that will make the heroine impervious to male sexuality, passion will provide its own antidote. As a result, sexuality becomes a tool for vengeance enacted on the villain, rather than the locus of fruitful conflict as it is in contemporary romance. The denial of sexuality, however, carries with it the denial of woman's power as a wife. For Lewis and Fleming, the heroine is an agent in her own destiny only while she remains single or estranged from her husband. And insofar as she manages to acquire real property and power, she does so specifically in the role of daughter, that is, as the presexual child who inherits the patrimony.

Thus, power, in the shape of money, passes hands in these earlier romances not through the sexual battle between hero and heroine, culminating in their eventual marriage, but through death. The insistence on estates and inheritance not only functions as a displacement of the marketplace economy, but as a fantasy of family conflict. Lewis, as we have seen, is especially transparent in her manipulation of these themes, but both writers insist on the passage of money from father to daughter, the father sometimes marginally disguised as grandfather or adoptive parent, or both. Money, then, is specifically vested in the patriarchy, and in the fantasy world of

---

Charlton; Fleming's women who succeed in the arts become not writers but artists, as in *The Actress' Daughter*, or singers, as in *Carried by Storm*.

Victorian romance, money—which is to say, power—is passed on not to the competing sons, one weak and the other evil, but to the heroic daughter. The death of the father is, of course, essential to the inheritance, but that bald theme must be softened. The heroine does not kill the father; she brings about, instead, the death of his surrogate—her evil brother, the villain.

Contemporary romance fiction grants the heroine sexual fulfillment, marriage, and access to power, all three incorporated in the figure of the hero. But the Victorian romance distributes these aspects of fantasy fulfillment among villain, hero, and surrogate father, respectively. Moreover, through the defeat of the villain and the vitiation of the hero, these fictions make it plain that the fantasy gratification of these stories lies neither in sexual fulfillment nor married love. For Fleming and Lewis, and presumably their readers, pleasure lies in power, specifically in the appropriation of the patrimony directly at its patriarchal source.

4

WOMEN'S WORK

In spite of her fragile appearance,
[the heroine] is independent, high-spirited and
not too subservient. . . . Often she is starting a career,
leaving college, unhappy with her present job, or too caught up
in her work. . . . Though she wants to work, and plans to after
marriage, (in some business with her husband),
her home and children will always come first.

Guidelines, Silhouette Books

$\mathcal{T}$he heroine of Victorian romance acquires power directly, intruding herself into the line of patrilinear inheritance and avenging herself on patriarchal power in the character of the villain. Marriage in the stories of May Agnes Fleming and Harriet Lewis represents no more than the requisite formulaic closure with its halfhearted metamorphosis of the triumphant heroine into the conventional Victorian wife. But the heroine of contemporary romance can no longer gain power independently; instead, returning to an older convention, she must acquire wealth and status through marriage. The goal of this heroine is to find the right husband, the mature, successful, sensual hero. The problem for the heroine, of course, is that she cannot openly pursue this goal, that she must appear to be doing something else entirely. And in contemporary romance what the heroine must appear to be doing is working.

Despite the obsessive focus on passion and love in contemporary romance, it is still necessary to establish some other action, even minimal, for the story. Like her Victorian sister, the Harlequin heroine must be situated in what passes for the real world.[1] She must exist as a member of a class, with parents, dead or alive, rich or poor. She must also have a purpose, an activity, something that defines her and, more important, that gives her the appearance of something to do, something other than seeking marriage. In contemporary romance, work serves as a shorthand definition of status; heroines are typically introduced in terms of the work they do— very often work that marks a new period in their lives and accounts for their socioeconomic situation.

The heroines of Victorian sensational romance work too, but in the novels of Fleming and Lewis work functions differently, introducing a period of employment as the symbolic first step toward

1. For a fine discussion of the mixing of mythic and mimetic narration in popular romance and on the effects of this technique, see Janice Radway, *Reading the Romance: Women, Patriarchy, and Popular Literature* (Chapel Hill: University of North Carolina Press, 1984), pp. 186–208.

the heroine's independent achievement of economic success. The experience of the Victorian heroine in the world of work is an uneasy compromise between realism and fantasy, contemporaneity and anachronism. The absence of both the hero and the villain from the marketplace makes clear the futility, at least in practical terms, of this kind of economic enterprise; this is not where fortunes lie. But the heroine's ability to survive there, if not to prosper, gives her a set of credentials denied the male characters. The hero, as we have seen, maintains his purity at the expense of his virility by absenting himself altogether from economic competition. The villain employs his economic energy in pursuing the patrimony, thereby demonstrating his viciousness. The heroine, however, chooses the thornier path of paid employment, the path that popular nineteenth-century culture recommended for young American men. But this is woman's fantasy, not Horatio Alger's, and in the end the heroine, having demonstrated her economic virtue as a wage earner, is rewarded with the inherited wealth her virtue—if not her labor—has earned her. As a result, these Victorian heroines snatch a double economic triumph from men: in a nod to realism, they demonstrate the courage to enter the workplace, and, in the victory of romance, they inherit the family fortune.

The fictions of Harriet Lewis and May Agnes Fleming are certainly not unique in depicting the struggles of young women forced to earn a living. In *Victorian Working Women*, Wanda Neff notes that the Victorians discovered the working woman "as an object of pity, and in the literature of the early nineteenth century one first finds her portrayed as a victim of long hours, unfavourable conditions, and general injustice, for whom something ought to be done."[2] But Victorian romance is not concerned with the sociology of working women. If "something ought to be done" for these women, the solution of romance is the rescue through inheritance, the escape into fantasy.

Although the Victorian heroines of Fleming and Lewis engage

2. Wanda Fraiken Neff, *Victorian Working Women: An Historical and Literary Study of Women in British Industries and Professions, 1832–1850* (New York: AMS Press, 1966), p. 12.

in work only as a necessary, and symbolic, stage in their journey toward economic success through inheritance, work had a much greater value in itself for these writers, and for Fleming especially. For them, the real value of work was that it made it possible for women to remain single, and Fleming heartily approved of the single state. Although convention insisted that marriage had to be the destiny of her heroines, Fleming took pleasure in allowing some of her secondary characters more freedom of choice. Introducing a minor character in *Guy Earlscourt's Wife*, Fleming comments, "I hold her up before you in a glow of honest pride—a woman who was an old maid pure and simple from *choice*."[3] In *The Heir of Charlton*, Eleanor Charlton is conspicuously paraded before eligible men by her matrimony-minded mother. Humiliated by her mother's shamelessness, Eleanor pleads, "'I will work until I drop dead from work, I will lie down and die of starvation, before I marry any man for his money, and his money alone.'" At the end of the novel, from which she has disappeared for hundreds of pages, we find Eleanor again, now the principal of a young ladies' seminary in New Orleans: "She looks a strong and self-reliant woman sitting here, brave as well as gentle, sufficient unto herself, one who has, unaided, made a niche for herself in the world, and fits it well. She has the look of one who need not merge and lose her own individuality in that of any man."[4]

Such women may well be Fleming's personal real heroines, but they cannot serve as the heroines for her stories, where matrimony places the conventional seal on the acquisition of money and power. For those heroines, the typical locale for work is not the seminary, but the city, London or New York, where employment opportunities, restricted enough in the real world, are even more inhibited by the formulas of romance.

In setting their heroines to work, Lewis and Fleming were constrained by two sets of competing social values. Conventional female norms operate insofar as they limit the heroines to some form of

3. May Agnes Fleming, *Guy Earlscourt's Wife* (New York: G. W. Carleton, 1873), p. 47.
4. May Agnes Fleming, *The Heir of Charlton* (New York: G. W. Carleton, 1879), pp. 19, 383.

domestic employment. Needlework is a favored choice, combining a feminine activity with appallingly low pay, as is work in other people's houses, as a governess or a companion. To be sure, work associated with domestic chores does not represent any sudden allegiance to domestic values for Lewis and Fleming. It does, however, protect their heroines' class status, which jobs in stores and factories would have jeopardized, particularly in a period when immigrant women were entering the job force.[5]

At the same time, domestic work disassociates these heroines from employment that expresses excessive individualism and materialism. Whatever economic aggression the Victorian romances permits and celebrates, in the fantasy of feudal inheritances, there can be no such economic self-seeking in the real world of business and no possibility of self-realization through entrepreneurial success, for that is too closely associated with forms of masculine self-aggrandizement. But if male bourgeois goals are outlawed for the heroines of these romances, male bourgeois values of independence and economic self-sufficiency are vigorously upheld. No romance heroine is ever

5. Mary Ryan notes that between 1880 and 1910 the female work force was largely foreign born (*Womanhood in America: From Colonial Times to the Present*, 3d ed. [New York: Franklin Watts, 1983], p. 169). It should be noted that in choosing domestic employment for their heroines, Fleming and Lewis were reflecting real social conditions, for domestic work remained the principal form of female employment throughout the nineteenth century. See Julie A. Matthaei, *An Economic History of Women in America: Women's Work, the Sexual Division of Labor, and the Development of Capitalism* (New York: Schocken Books, 1982), p. 54. Carl Degler says that "throughout the 19th century the single largest occupation of women was domestic service," and notes that in 1880 45 percent of working women were employed as servants and laundresses alone (*At Odds: Women and the Family in America from the Revolution to the Present* [New York: Oxford University Press, 1980], pp. 372, 377). In analyzing women's employment between 1880 and 1930, Alice Kessler-Harris places it in the contexts of "virtue," "women's sense of being as it emerges from her 'naturally' prescribed roles," and "independence," "women's attempt to achieve without regard for family constraints." In such a construct, the heroines of Fleming and Lewis can be seen as expressing "virtue" in the marketplace and "independence" in their successful competition for feudal inheritances. Kessler-Harris also notes that "notions of propriety" defined women's jobs "in terms of values appropriate to future home life" ("Independence and Virtue in the Lives of Wage-Earning Women: The United States, 1870–1930," in *Women in Culture and Politics: A Century of Change*, ed. Judith Friedlander, Blanche Wiesen Cook, Alice Kessler-Harris, and Carroll Smith-Rosenberg [Bloomington: Indiana University Press, 1986], pp. 4, 9).

cold or hungry enough even to consider falling back on charity. Thus, impoverished, but genteel and proud, the heroines struggle through under the double burden of conflicting male and female values.[6]

When the heroine is forced to become a governess, romance novels, like other Victorian fiction, show that life to be intolerable. Employed by a woman too stingy to provide her room and board and too haughty to treat her with kindness, Harriet Lewis's Beryl grows weak and ill from lack of adequate food and must attempt to supplement her wages with needlework.[7] Even when the family is kind and generous, as in Fleming's *The Actress' Daughter*, Georgia Darrell suffers inordinately from depression and the loss of autonomy.[8] Work as a companion, however, serves a different function. Such employment loses its connection with realism and provides a bridge to the fantasy resolution of romance. The heroine becomes companion to an elderly gentleman, and he is either discovered to be the heroine's father or grandfather, as in *Beryl's Husband*, or he chooses to adopt her because of her goodness to him, as in *Norine's Revenge*. In Fleming's *Her Double Life*, both outcomes occur, the grandfather of the heroine adopting her as his niece.[9]

The hardships a Victorian heroine faces in the world of work, however, are trivial compared to the horrors potential in the domestic servitude suffered by dependent girls or unhappy wives. Fleming creates her most powerful scenes when she depicts women and girls enslaved in brutal households and allows these characters to retaliate with violent acts of frustration and revenge. The heroine of *Carried by Storm* is twelve when the story opens; apparently an orphan, she lives at Sleaford Farm, brutalized by overwork and cruelty.

6. Matthaei emphasizes the connection between economic success and self-realization: "Under capitalism, men's striving in the economy becomes, literally, a seeking of their selves, a struggle to establish their own identities by competing with other men" (*Economic History of Women*, p. 103).

7. Harriet Lewis, *Beryl's Husband* (1874; New York: Robert Bonner's Sons, 1891).

8. May Agnes Fleming, *The Actress' Daughter* (New York: G. W. Carleton, 1886).

9. Lewis, *Beryl's Husband*; May Agnes Fleming, *Norine's Revenge* (New York: G. W. Carleton, 1875); Harriet Lewis, *Her Double Life* (New York: Robert Bonner's Sons, 1883).

"Sleaford's Joanna," as she is called, is no Cinderella, melancholy but patient. She is closer to a wild child. We meet her when the other, more conventional heroine, herself a child, becomes lost in the woods. Joanna finds her, terrifies her with threats, extorts from her her gold necklace, and threatens to cut off her long golden hair. Joanna torments the other child in the language of class warfare:

> "She wants to go home? Oh, she wants to go home! Oh! please somebody come and take this young lady home! . . . What business have you, you stuck-up little peacock! . . . with hair down to your waist, yellow hair too . . . and all in nasty ringlets! Oh, lordy! we think ourselves handsome, don't we? . . . And a kerridge to ride it! . . . We're a great lady, *we* are. . . . do you know that I hate you, that I would like to tramp on you, that I spit at you! . . . I hate you because you're a young lady, with kerridges, and servants, and nothin' to do, and long yellow ringlets down your stuck-up back."[10]

Eventually, Joanna runs off to the city, reveling in her freedom and prepared to look for housework to support herself. But Fleming lets her off this requisite stint at humble employment, partly because she has already put in adequate time at suffering and partly because her very willingness to do domestic work exonerates her from the charge of living in fantasy. She is not "one of those foolish, romance-reading country girls who run away from home and come to New York to seek their fortunes . . . the fortune they mostly find is ruin and sin for life, and a death of dark despair."[11] Joanna works hard, earning very little money, but she is working as a singer, developing herself as an artist.

In *Who Wins?* it is the wife whom we see in domestic servility, tormented, beaten. The story opens when she is on the road with her husband and baby. Exhausted, she pleads that they stop in the town ahead, but he refuses, cursing and threatening her: " 'You want me to beat in that white face of yours to jelly—don't you?' " At last

10. May Agnes Fleming, *Carried by Storm* (1879; New York: G. W. Carleton, 1880), pp. 30–31.
11. Ibid., p. 192.

he hits her a brutal blow between the eyes, so that she staggers back, "the blood spurting." At nightfall, he leaves her and the child by a tree while he goes to get himself some drink. When he returns, drunk, he forces her to spend the night outdoors in a storm. It is too much; she has been driven too far. Her husband falls into a drunken sleep and she picks up "a long, sharp-pointed stone, deadly as a dagger," and "struck him with all her might upon the temple. There was one convulsive bound, one gurgling cry, a spout of hot, red blood, and then—" [12]

For Fleming, violence and cruelty serve to dramatize her view of the unpaid domestic labor of dependent girl or dependent wife as the most degrading form of women's work. The value of paid labor, no matter how menial, is that it provides women some recourse to economic security other than marriage. Marriage is a perilous state, always a condition of potential bondage. Rose Dawson, the murderous wife, and Sleaford's Joanna, each of them in a state of domestic servitude, lack even the minimal independence attendant on hard work at low pay. And Fleming would not have seen much differ-ence in their situations; the conditions of brutalized girl and brutal-ized wife come down to the same thing: dependence. An important function of work for Fleming's heroines is that it provides an ap-prenticeship in independence and that, almost as surely as economic power, helps protect women from the peril and potential violence of marriage and domestic life.

The ferocity of Fleming's depictions of the dark world of domestic enslavement breaks out in episodes of unrestrained violence. Given the conventions of fiction, of course, violence cannot go unpunished, but Fleming finds it difficult to tie the requisite punishment directly to the violent acts her language seems to relish. As a result, the nar-rative logic of punishment is tortured. Thus, the murderous wife of *Who Wins?* is transformed in a single chapter into a beautiful actress who dazzles an aristocratic young man into marriage. As seductress, she is evil, allied to the villain, enmeshed in plots. But her emer-gence as an evil woman and the punishment the novel finally inflicts

12. May Agnes Fleming, *Who Wins? or, The Secret of Monkswood* (1870; New York: The New York Book Company, 1910), pp. 3–4.

on her are justified not by her act of murder but by her seduction of the young hero. Fleming even allows one of her characters to explain this to the actress: " 'You're a clever little woman, Rose, and I rather admire your pluck in putting an end to that drunken beast Dawson; but, by Jove! when you delude infatuated young men into marrying you, you come it a little strong.' " [13]

On the other hand, perhaps because her crimes stop short of either murder or entrapment, Joanna, the heroine of *Carried by Storm*, is finally redeemed from the wretchedness of her life. To be sure, she does not marry the hero; that is reserved for the poor blonde child she tormented in the woods. But marrying the hero is not, as we have seen, a particularly telling victory in itself. As for Joanna, she becomes a famous singer, finds that she is an heiress, rediscovers her mother—and as a distinct afterthought marries Sir Roland Hardwicke. Her emergence as Lady Hardwicke is mentioned at the very close of the story; we have never before even heard Sir Roland's name.

Despite its symbolic importance, work as a practical endeavor is a dead end for Victorian romance heroines. But work was a dead end for most women at that time. Serious American fiction tells the same story about work and women, emphasizing its futility but omitting the fantasy resolution, the rescue by the fairy godfather. Serious American fiction, in fact, typically retells the story Joanna escapes in *Carried by Storm*. Unlike other foolish runaway girls in New York, Joanna is properly realistic in her goals, prepared to do housework rather than futilely seek some glamorous employment. Such expectations, as her landlady warns, lead to the old story of "ruin and sin," followed by a "death of dark despair." In Stephen Crane's hands that is precisely Maggie's brief and brutal story. But in other examples, like Dreiser's *Sister Carrie* or David Graham Phillips's *Susan Lennox*, ruin and sin become the road to financial success, whatever terminal melancholy is said to envelop the rich and independent heroine.[14]

13. Ibid., p. 20.

14. Apparently, the possibilities for recovery after "ruin and sin" seemed distinctly limited to Dreiser and Phillips; both Carrie and Susan Lennox succeed in the

The significant aspect of these Victorian romances is not only that they provide a fantasy rescue for the heroine, but that they show her surviving *without* recourse to ruin and sin, that they give her a brief period of independence and self-reliance. Through that demonstration of independence the Victorian romance heroine proves her mettle in a man's world and provides evidence of her worthiness for economic rescue.

Independence notwithstanding, the heroine of Victorian romance cannot become rich in the marketplace. Richardson's *Pamela*, not Defoe's *Moll Flanders*, becomes the model for female upward mobility, and even the aggressive heroine that Fleming and Lewis create cannot afford so direct a challenge to her essential womanliness. Moll Flanders can make money and marry, and marry, and marry, in the end living happily ever after with the man she loves. After *Moll Flanders* a woman's ability to succeed in the marketplace invalidates her for romantic success. Making money defeminizes the heroine.

Contemporary romance has until very recently described the daughters of Moll Flanders with the opprobrious epithet, "liberated." But even the unliberated woman in contemporary romance has not been relieved from the necessity of work. The problem for today's romance fictions is to find something for the heroine to do, but the question of what kind of work is a good deal more perplexing for contemporary romance writers than for their Victorian predecessors. The very fact that work is more available and potentially more rewarding for women than it was a century ago creates difficulties for popular romance. On the one hand, a heroine who clerks in a five-and-ten is unsatisfactory; she has too little personal ambition and her job makes her too subservient. But a heroine who heads a corporation is no better; she has too much ambition and her job identifies her as too domineering and masterful. In choosing the heroine's work, the romance writer must walk a very narrow line: work must appear meaningful enough to absorb the heroine's interest, keeping her mind off marriage, and at the same time not so meaningful that she would either prefer it to marriage

theater, suggesting that a career as actress was marginal enough, socially, to provide an acceptable solution to the novelists' problems.

or want to continue to pursue it independently after marriage. For the Victorian romance, work is a necessary experience, a formulaic stint at independence. For the contemporary romance, work is a necessary deception; at the very least, it must fool the heroine into averting her eyes from her real lifework—finding a husband.

At the same time, the romance heroine's work represents a complex response both to ideology and to social reality. Of course, popular attitudes toward women's work and the actual conditions of women's employment are mutually self-enforcing, especially in more conservative segments of society. Secretarial work or school teaching, for example, are not only realistic forms of employment; they also reinforce conventional female roles and values. Whether as Girl Friday or substitute mother, the heroine enacts her womanly role.[15] Nevertheless, the choice of work presents problems precisely because the conservative view has been challenged by feminism and because some women have recently made gains in business and the professions. As a result, the very choice of a heroine's employment necessarily becomes a political statement.

Recently, contemporary romance has offered a response to feminism, at least insofar as feminism has insisted on real careers for women and on work as self-defining and self-creating for women, as it has long been for men. Heroines of some romances, as a result, appear as corporate heads but, as we shall see, any consequent self-definition on the heroine's part turns out all wrong. The liberated heroine fails to know herself, for self-realization continues to be entirely a sexual issue.

15. Alice Kessler-Harris sees "a generation of repressed ambition" released in the 1960s, resulting in an undermining of earlier conceptions of proper women's work, even work in the shape of careers. Before the 1960s, she writes, "careers in nursing, libraries, teaching, and social work drew on years of socialization and a consciousness bred to serve" ("*Independence and Virtue*," p. 14). Evidence suggests, however, that despite the 1960s, women's work is still largely defined by these more traditional ideas. By the late 1970s, according to Mary Ryan, when half of all women were in the work force, "Nearly half of these new women workers, some 5 million in number, settled for low-level jobs." Clerical work, especially, like domestic work in the nineteenth century, had become "a virtual ghetto of women workers," with 80 percent of all clerical positions held by women (*Womanhood in America*, pp. 317–19). Carl Degler states that by the mid-1970s women were largely in the same work categories as in 1900 (*At Odds*, p. 423).

By no means, of course, do all forms of work challenge old assumptions, insist on the independence of the heroine, or pose a threat, even temporarily, to the power of sexuality and love. Some romances, indeed, go very far in denying any such assertiveness; in a curious echo of Victorian romance, some heroines turn to domestic work. Domestic employment dramatically denies independence and negates even modest ambition in the heroine, which makes it a useful device; but by the same token it suggests a heroine so modest and potentially so subservient that it has to be motivated very carefully.

In some cases the contemporary heroine who becomes a domestic worker does so in disguise, as if to protect herself from the charge of weakness and excessive submission and to give her some other, secret identity at once more assertive and more glamorous. Daphne Clair's *Never Count Tomorrow* uses this device and, paradoxically, makes domestic work a step toward personal independence. The wealthy heroine Melinda wants independence from her father's money and therefore answers an advertisement for housekeeper and "childminder" in Paikea, a remote area of New Zealand. Melinda finds a benign environment. Teresa, the widow who employs her, shares the work with her, and only Soren, Teresa's stepson and the hero, ever insists on her role as hired help. At the same time, Melinda proves herself a willing and able worker. No spoiled daughter of the rich, "she worked harder than anyone expected or demanded of her, cleaning, polishing, and scrubbing. . . . [Melinda] had an obsession—no one would be able to say she didn't earn the good wage she was getting for this."[16] The rewards for hard work are considerable, for Melinda ends up with the hero and with a new family, finding in Teresa a surrogate mother.

Not all domestic work is so benign. *The Little Impostor* by Lilian Peake brings Cara Hirst into a household where work as a companion calls for the eradication of her personality. In order to earn money rapidly so that she and her fiancé can marry, Cara resigns her job as a history teacher and finds a position as companion to a rich

16. Daphne Clair, *Never Count Tomorrow* (Toronto: Harlequin Books, 1980), p. 27.

old woman confined to a wheelchair. The old woman's demands are bizarre and even sadistic. Cara must cut her hair off and wear at all times a uniform that consists of a "drab navy-blue coat, navy lace-up shoes, white blouse with its demure collar and thick, straight, navy skirt." Her appearance is to be emblematic of her attitude, one of " 'docility . . . meekness . . . obedience.' " And she is always a servant, never treated as a member of the family. The old woman tells her that " 'whatever social position you may have held before coming to work for me, here, in my employment, you are in a very subordinate position indeed.' " [17]

Once attractive, Cara is rendered plain, with the purpose of denying her any sexual allure. The old woman has stipulated that her companion must have no male friend, " 'no young man, no thoughts of marriage in mind.' " She wants a companion who will remain with her, who will see the job as " 'a pensionable occupation.' " She is rich and can promise that her companion will " 'inherit from me more—far more than you ever dreamed of possessing.' " If the situation is Victorian in its echoes of a single woman's permanent thralldom in another woman's household, so too is the promise of power through money the old woman holds out to Cara: " 'Believe me, it will be better than a husband, it will bring you more happiness, more satisfaction and more worldly goods than any man could ever give you.' " [18] But Cara is a contemporary heroine and cannot pursue money as a discrete goal; nor can she inherit her employer's money in order to bestow her new wealth on the hero. Cara achieves riches by marrying the old woman's rich and famous nephew.

The most frequent kind of domestic work for contemporary romance heroines occurs with marriage, not the marriage that ends each story, but the early marriage that provides so popular a variant for romance fiction. A major function of the early marriage story, as we have seen, is to permit sexual consummation not typically allowed to unmarried heroines. But early marriage also operates to

17. Lilian Peake, *The Little Impostor* (Toronto: Harlequin Books, 1977), pp. 16, 11, 20.
18. Ibid., pp. 27, 31–32.

negate the heroine's quasi-independent status. The heroine is never allowed to establish a home; she is always taken into the hero's domestic world, not quite a captive, but certainly a constrained dependent.

Early marriage in contemporary romance does not focus on domestic work; it is not a question of washing dishes and making beds. The hero is rich and the heroine's problem, along with accommodating herself to sex and learning to deal with her hidden love for the hero, is to remake herself into a proper wife for so prosperous and powerful a man. Here, too, we have an echo of a Victorian theme. In *The Actress' Daughter*, Wildair tells Georgia Darrell, his new wife, that she must lose her " 'country girl awkwardness' " and learn to " 'do the honors of my house as becomes one whom I have seen fit to raise to the position of my wife.' "[19] In contemporary romance, however, the hero need not say this himself; the example of the elegant, sophisticated, and worldly Other Woman makes it clear enough to the heroine.

Engineering early marriage takes some ingenuity. In Amii Lorin's *Morgan Wade's Woman*, the heroine is forced to marry by the terms of her father's will, terms that one character labels "Victorian." A more typical device is the orphaned child, one for whom both hero and heroine feel responsible. In *Season of Shadows* by Yvonne Whittal, ten-year-old Sally is orphaned when her parents' pleasure boat explodes at sea. Sally's only relative is her Aunt Laura, but her guardian is the wealthy Anton DeVere. DeVere insists on keeping Sally, for with his money he can raise her properly. Sally loves Anton but cannot bear to have Aunt Laura leave her. Her hysteria necessitates a visit from the doctor whose prescription is clear enough: " 'There's no doubt in my mind that she's extremely fond of both you *and* Anton, and to part from either of you at this crucial time might unbalance her completely, I'm afraid.' "[20]

Caroline Franklin, of Jeanne Stephens's *Wonder and Wild Desire*, is responsible for supporting her ten-month-old orphaned nephew,

19. Fleming, *The Actress' Daughter*, p. 189.
20. Yvonne Whittal, *Season of Shadows* (Toronto: Harlequin Books, 1980), p. 38.

Mike, but as the story opens, she has just lost her job. At that point, Joshua Revell appears; having discovered the existence of his brother's illegitimate child, he wants custody of him. Although she is unable to support Mike, Caroline cannot part with him. Revell comes up with the solution: marriage. When Caroline resists, he presses the argument: " 'Even if you can manage financially until you find another job, you can't afford to fight me in court. And think about the baby. Do you really want to raise an illegitimate child? Consider how that could affect him when he's old enough to understand.' " [21] Like the heroine of *Season of Shadows*, Caroline finds that her love for a child outweighs her powerful aversion to the hero; marriage seems a reasonable sacrifice. The hero, however, always has two motives. As we learn at the resolution of each such story, he loves not only the child but, from the outset, the heroine as well.

Early-marriage stories, however they are engineered, provide a particularly rich fantasy in the opportunity they afford for more explicitly developed love scenes. Moreover, the substitution of marriage for some other kind of work adds another kind of gratification. The heroine may find it difficult to fit herself into the hero's grand style, but it is not at all difficult to enjoy it. Early-marriage stories are replete with servants, fine clothes, and gifts of extraordinary jewels and furs, gifts no self-respecting single girl could accept. These stories give a foretaste of the pleasures of money.

Romances that engage the heroine in domestic work, either as hired help or unwilling bride, entirely avoid the problems associated with careers in the marketplace, for in these stories the heroine's work is not something she has chosen, but something forced on her by what passes for necessity. A real career proves more problematic. One popular solution to the problem of a suitable career lies in the arts, a neat accommodation of the idea of commitment to the necessity of steering clear of the negative associations attached to the marketplace. This is not a new idea, of course, for Fleming and Lewis occasionally use the same device, not only for their heroines—allowed to succeed as painters or singers—but in Flem-

21. Jeanne Stephens, *Wonder and Wild Desire* (New York: Simon and Schuster, Silhouette Books, 1981), p. 31.

108

ing's case for her heroes who, as writers, demonstrate their ability to succeed outside of the corrupting economic arena.

Even with the arts, however, some restraint on ambition is usually necessary. Although romances do occasionally paint heroines who are talented and committed artists,[22] the majority are a good deal less assertive in their claims. The more typical artistic heroine has limited ambitions or limited success—or even limited talent. The art student in Brooke Hastings's *Innocent Fire* is first a student of the hero, an internationally famous painter, but before long she becomes his model. Tiana Spencer of Paula Edwards's *Bewitching Grace*, an aspiring commercial artist, is transformed into a model, too. She finds, moreover, that the real world is less than receptive to her large ambition and small experience. Applying for a position as staff artist in an advertising agency, the job she ends up with is photographer's assistant.[23] Kate Brown, in Dixie Browning's *East of Today*, was trained as a watercolorist, a rather modest artistic assertion. She has worked as a high school teacher and in the story we find her trying to start a school in watercolor painting. Analogous modesty inherent in the very kind of art pursued appears with Laura Sloane of Charlotte Lamb's *Retribution*, who is a writer but a writer of children's books. Failure, finally, makes its own statement: Jane Larue of Violet Winspear's *A Girl Possessed*, an actress, but an unemployed actress.[24]

Success in the arts is relatively rare in romance, but it is a possibility. Success in the marketplace proper has only very recently become acceptable, for typically popular romance finds success

22. Examples include the heroine of *Flamenco Nights* who will continue her painting even after marriage, pianist Nicole Swithin of *The Tempestuous Lovers*, and Clarissa Harlowe of *New Discovery*, who is a prize-winning novelist. Susanna Collins, *Flamenco Nights* (New York: Jove Books, Second Chance at Love, 1981); Suzanne Simmons, *The Tempestuous Lovers* (New York: Dell, Candlelight Ecstasy Romance, 1981); Jessica Ayre, *New Discovery* (Toronto: Harlequin Romances, 1984).

23. Brooke Hastings, *Innocent Fire* (New York: Simon and Schuster, Silhouette Romance, 1980); Paula Edwards, *Bewitching Grace* (New York: Simon and Schuster, Silhouette Romance, 1980).

24. Dixie Browning, *East of Today* (New York: Simon and Schuster, Silhouette Romance, 1981); Charlotte Lamb, *Retribution* (Toronto: Harlequin Books, 1981); Violet Winspear, *A Girl Possessed* (Toronto: Harlequin Books, 1981).

in the business world prima facie evidence of "liberation." Contemporary romance writers, like Fleming and Lewis before them, have been suspicious of the marketplace, but unlike the Victorians, today's romance writers no longer express a wholesale mistrust of the real economic world. That world continues to threaten to corrupt women, but it no longer holds any evil associations for men. Contemporary heroes are frequently portrayed as giants of the marketplace, now accepted in popular romance as the arena for male acquisition of power. For a woman to succeed there, however, remains dangerous, threatening the loss of her womanliness. In most contemporary romances the "liberated woman" is defeminized, lost between two genders. When she appears at all in the role of heroine, it becomes the responsibility of the hero to reclaim her.

A very straightforward example of this hostility to the successful career woman is *Liberated Lady* by Sally Wentworth. Sara has made a successful career in advertising. An early romantic affair ended when she discovered that her fiancé was frivolous with his time and money; moreover, she was promoted ahead of him and "it had hurt dreadfully that he wasn't man enough to take her success." She is ambitious and "very keen" on her work. At the same time she is motivated by the need to earn money to support her younger half sister, a motivation that provides evidence of some smoldering ashes of womanliness. When the hero meets her, and they instantly quarrel, he calls her "one of the most dictatorial and unfeminine women I've ever had the misfortune to meet." He goes on to make his criticism of her a class action. "'You career women are all the same—you're so busy beating men down in your fight to get to the top that you lose all your femininity.'" Apparently, the reader should accept this indictment, for the story finds the hero successfully taming Sara the shrew. Against the general formulaic material of sexual dominance a countertheme plays, insisting on Sara's personal and emotional jeopardy as a cold career woman. When the hero, a hundred pages earlier than the formula requires, declares his love, it is Sara who refuses to confess hers. When she can no longer deny her feelings and accepts his proposal of marriage, she does so only on the condition that she continue working: "'I *need* to work. . . . I'm used to the stimulus.'" But he wants a "'full-time wife . . . not someone who's tired out in the evenings and can think of nothing but the problems she's got to face the next day.'"[25]

Liberated Lady insists on the defeminization of the career woman, even introducing a remarkable shift in gender roles in regard to sex and marriage. The masculine heroine, refusing to give up her career but still desiring the hero, offers to live with him. Although the hero has made it clear that he "'want[s] a wife not a mistress,'" he pretends to go along, thinking that if he treats her as no more than a sex object, she will see they must marry—and on his terms. Instead, they quarrel and part again. When they next meet, Sara thinks about her problem.

> Knowing him had taught her a lot; that she wasn't willing to sacrifice her career and her independence for marriage and security, and also that she couldn't blithely enter into a cold-blooded sexual relationship. So just what did she want? she wondered wryly. A man who would be warm and loving, but otherwise not make any demands on her time and her freedom, someone who stayed conveniently in the background? She smiled cynically to herself; that sounded much more like a wife than a husband.

Although Sara's cynical acknowledgment of the conventional role of women in marriage adds some ambiguity to the story's general dismantling of women's liberation, and although the hero declares in the final scene that he had fallen in love with Sara "'for the very qualities I was trying to make you give up,'" *Liberated Lady* embraces a rigidly conventional view of women's appropriate roles. Sara is shrill and shrewish until the end, alienated not only from the hero but from the other sympathetic characters, including her own half sister. Even the apparent solution to the dilemma of marriage and career enforces the dominance of the conventional view of women. Although the hero offers Sara a position as his "'part-time Public

25. Sally Wentworth, *Liberated Lady* (Toronto: Harlequin Books, 1979), pp. 26, 17, 19.

Relations office,'" he immediately undercuts it with the mocking observation that "'there is one small drawback—you'll have to sleep with the boss.'"[26]

The scenes of sexual arousal in *Liberated Lady* are no different from those in other contemporary romances, but the language of dominance assumes new overtones in the context of the career woman. The hero's success in enforcing his will sexually now translates into his ability to minimize or even eradicate the heroine's professional ambitions. Since the heroine's career aspirations are understood as stunting her womanliness, her latent sexuality, the hero's role here simply carries through the logic of the narrative. Other stories that take on, if less directly, the question of the liberated woman also causally link her economic success with sexual failure. Such stories place professional and sexual self-realization in competition, as if vying for a discreet and finite source of energy. Moreover, the depletion of this stock of energy cannot be easily reversed, for after a time the heroine's latent sexuality may atrophy, her commitment to a career extinguishing even her potential for passion.[27] The heroine in *East of Today* suspects "there was something obviously missing in her makeup, and she sighed now as she wondered if she were being a silly, romantic fool for even dreaming of anything more." In part her problem comes from her current boyfriend, weak and unsensual, but in part it results from her own life choices up to this point. As the hero says when Kate recoils from the power of her sexual response to him, "'you've left it too long now, I'm afraid. You'll never be more than half a woman.'"[28]

The interplay between career and sexuality undergoes significant modification, however, in those newer romances that feature a

26. Ibid., pp. 152, 173–74, 182, 186.

27. It is worth commenting that this competition for energy neatly displaces a more conventional concern over women's abilities to maintain a family and a career simultaneously, functions that compete for time. Mary Ryan traces the home-career polarity in the twentieth century, from the twenties when career opportunities opened up for women but were still seen as the province of single women or of married women before and after child rearing, through the fifties when social theory, especially as influenced by Talcott Parsons, redrew "the line between home and society" (*Womanhood in America*, pp. 248, 260).

28. Browning, *East of Today*, pp. 42, 108.

heroine who competes in a man's world and does so successfully. This new approach to the romance heroine's work, however hedged about with special conditions and caveats, requires some adjustments in the conception of the heroine herself and in the way the romance formula is carried out. The basic formula, nonetheless, is unchanged. The heroine meets the hero, is sexually attracted to him, and goes through a period of conflict and tension as a result of the hero's apparent rejection of all but her sexual self. The heroine's acknowledgment of her love for the hero only intensifies her sense of weakness and misery until the story is resolved in the hero's confession of his love for her. The changes that occur within the formula as a result of accommodating it to the successful career woman are primarily changes that affect the locus of the conflict and, secondarily, the presentation of the hero.

The conventional conflict in contemporary romance lies initially between the hero and heroine as a sexual struggle and subsequently becomes internalized in the heroine. With the development of the heroine as an independent career woman, the conflict takes on another dimension, becoming a struggle between career and love as well as between sexual passion and love. Like the conflict between sex and love, the tension between career and love becomes internalized in the heroine. The issue is one of competing energies as the arousal of her own sexuality forces her to see that, as a career woman, she is not a complete person, not a "real" woman, and that she can only become a real woman through the acknowledgment and development of this newly discovered sexual aspect of herself. In a conventional romance like *Liberated Lady*, the heroine learns to become a woman by allowing love to triumph over career, but some recent stories are more generous with the heroine, permitting her to achieve love and to maintain her independent career. The successful resolution of these fictions, like those in more conventional romances, continues to depend on the transformation of the hero. As always, he must learn to value love and to subdue the energy of passion to the restraints of love. But beyond that, he must also come to recognize that the heroine's career is of value and that, in fact, she is the woman he loves precisely because of her professional commitment and competence.

The widened locus of conflict in romances with career women as heroines and the consequent adjustments in the means of resolving the conflict demand a somewhat altered version of the hero. The essential aspects of his character, of course, remain intact; he is older, successful, masterful, sexual, and domineering. But he is no longer the macho hero of much conventional romance. His principle task is still to awaken the heroine to sexuality, but because the conflict is no longer the simple struggle between sexuality and love, it is no longer appropriate, or even adequate, to have a hero who signifies the brute force of unleashed sexual passion. At the same time, since even the career-woman heroine must be emotionally destabilized by the hero, he must continue to exhibit behavior that the heroine finds unreadable: he must be moody, he must move incomprehensibly back and forth between seduction and rejection of the heroine. But if that behavior cannot be attributed to some generalized savage male principle, then it must be individually and psychologically motivated. In earlier romances it is not untypical to find heroes who have suffered from the actions of some woman earlier in their lives and who have, as a result, learned to distrust all women and to deny the possibility of love. In the romances that present the new career-minded heroine, however, *all* heroes have suffered at the hands of women; *all* heroes are psychologically wounded.

The wounded hero is vulnerable. The heroine is no longer the single victim in these stories, fighting her way from victimhood to triumph in love and marriage; now she has to share that role with the hero. Moreover, unlike more conventional forms of romance, the hero's wound is not something the heroine—and the reader— discover late in the novel as an ex post facto apology for his behavior. The hero's wound is presented early and presented frequently, kept before us as a way of underlining the idea that the hero and heroine are both engaged in the difficult process of maturing into love.

So important is this idea that it has led some romance writers to abandon the traditional narrative point of view for romance. Some recent stories substitute for the limited third-person narration that keeps the reader locked into the heroine's perceptions and emotions a point of view that shifts back and forth between heroine and hero. The effect of this change is startling. No longer is the hero's behavior left mysterious and unmotivated. The heroine may be desperately confused but the reader cannot be. Of course, the veteran romance reader always knows what the hero is up to anyway, understands that his savagery will be transmuted into love. But now the reader is forced to confront the hero as a character who is suffering, just like the heroine, and as a character who commands sympathy, just like the heroine.

In Joanna Scott's *Corporate Policy* the hero is a movie producer, rich, successful, and a notorious lady's man. We see him first through the heroine's eyes, as a threat to her emotional composure and to her career ambitions. But quite soon after that, as the narrative point of view shifts, we see him directly. We find that he has no self-esteem as a lover, admitting that he has really not done well in "the romance department" and acknowledging that his success with women has depended more on his importance in the movie industry than on his personal charms. His romantic conquests have been no more than "a parade of easily forgotten women who were too fascinated by their own beauty and careers to see him as anything but a giant step on their stairway to stardom." He had once become engaged to just such a woman and "never again would he mistake ambition for love." But his wound goes yet deeper; even his mother had betrayed him. He is, therefore, a lonely and suspicious man: "Only one woman had ever loved him—his grandmother. She was the only woman he trusted."[29]

It is not a question here of new material in the character of the hero; heroes of more conventional romances suffer similar betrayals. Rather, it is a matter of presentation: the reader is forced to confront the hero directly as a person whose self-doubt and suffering are every bit as significant as the heroine's. This hero's claim on our sympathy, moreover, in some ways exceeds that of the heroine, for his understanding and compassion are much deeper than hers. His suffering has created in him such sensitivity that he recognizes

29. Joanna Scott, *Corporate Policy* (New York: Simon and Schuster, Silhouette Books, 1984), p. 49.

in the heroine a loneliness and defensiveness similar to his own, empathically understanding that she had built around herself a "hard protective shell." [30]

The wounded hero is also generous spirited. Once he learns how deeply the heroine values her career, he certainly never asks her to give it up. In fact, it is usually the hero who finds a way to accommodate marriage and their two careers, especially difficult when geographical distance is a factor.

The hero of Faye Wildman's *The Fletcher Legacy* is especially accommodating. This story pits hero and heroine against one another in a conflict directly associated with business; nevertheless, they have no problem admitting their mutual attraction and, short of love, their mutual affection. When the business conflict is resolved, the hero and heroine are free to express their love, but the problem of two careers and two locales remains. Conveniently, the hero has been preparing to sell out his business in remote Preston Falls, for he has begun a novel and plans a new career as a writer. Thus, when the heroine tells him she cannot marry him because she cannot live in Preston Falls, he supplies the happy ending: " 'Who's asking you to live in Preston Falls? I wouldn't expect it of you. I got a good deal on the sale of my business, and we're going to buy a house just outside of Vancouver, within commuting distance for you, and I'm going to write my book while you go on being president of Fletcher Paper.' "

The Fletcher Legacy provides a particularly gratifying resolution to the problems the career woman creates for romance. " 'I can't believe you'd do all this for me,' " the heroine says, and the hero replies, as he hands her a "single solitaire sapphire, the color of the ocean. . . . 'I'd do anything in the world for you. Just ask me.' " [31]

30. Ibid., p. 50.
31. Faye Wildman, *The Fletcher Legacy* (New York: Simon and Schuster, Silhouette Books, 1984), pp. 184–85. Another example is Ariel Berk's *Promise of Love.* The heroine, Carla Roche, runs a casting agency in New York and falls in love with Bryce Dalton, a brilliant movie director who has his home and studio in San Francisco. In the final pages of the story, Bryce confesses his love and proposes, although he fears they may " 'wind up spending the rest of our lives flying back and forth across the country.' " But he has already thought of a solution: Carla can expand her

In the guise of career woman, the romance heroine assumes the task of developing her sexual, emotional nature while maintaining her career interests and her personal ambition. At the same time, she must modify her single-minded pursuit of her career, allowing room for sexual expression and ultimately for love and marriage. The resolution of the heroine's story brings her both love and work, but the unfolding of the story itself makes very clear how deep the conflict between love and work remains for romance fiction.

Corporate Policy fully exploits this conflict. Kate Howard is an insurance lawyer, brought up to expect that she would take over her father's business, Associated Insurance. But when he dies, she finds that her assets are in trust, and soon her stepmother, who controls the trust, sells the business to movie producer Grant Brawley, president of Worldwide Artists. Kate moves to the coast as general counsel to Associated Insurance, in other words as Grant's employee. Kate, however, provides no example of the submissive, selfless woman worker. In the first place, her goal is to gain control of her trust and buy back her father's company. And second, her conservative financial outlook causes her to oppose Grant's plans to use the money available from Associated to finance his movies. As in *The Fletcher Legacy*, the hero and heroine quickly acknowledge their mutual passion and soon their mutual need for one other, despite their antagonistic business goals. Each, however, remains deeply cautious, defensive, afraid to trust the other, their suspicion motivated both professionally and personally, for each has suffered at the hands of the other sex. Grant, as we saw above, had been wounded by his mother and his fiancee. Kate has been hurt by her father, jealous of his marriage to her stepmother and betrayed by the terms of his will. Since the two of them are continually engaged in a real struggle over the investment of Associated's funds and future control of seats on the board of directors, career and love are placed in violent opposition.

Grant proposes to Kate well before the novel closes, but it is clear that the price of marriage—the price of love—is Kate's sur-

business, leaving her associate in the New York office while she opens a West Coast branch [New York: Simon and Schuster, Silhouette Books, 1984], pp. 184–85).

render in the corporate struggle. She wants additional seats on the board of directors, but Grant argues that she doesn't need them if she is married to him: "'Don't you think I can take care of you?'" Kate, however, is unwilling to become dependent on him: "'The trust money, the stock and whatever goes with them are mine.'" The dialogue that follows highlights the conflict between career and marriage, specifically in terms of independence and love.

"And you'd use them against me, wouldn't you?" He had been a fool to trust her, to tell her he loved her.

"Don't be ridiculous. I love you. I wouldn't do anything to hurt you. I just want to control my own life. . . ."

"Ridiculous, am I, Kate? It's *our* life I'm talking about, not just yours. . . ."

Kate didn't answer. What could she say? That she would continue letting [her stepmother] manage her money? No way. Grant wanted her to trust him. What about trusting her? . . .

"So, controlling that damn company still means more to you than I do. Well, I don't intend to hover around your skirts while you try to destroy me. I'm warning you, Kate, come with me now, or it's all over between us. . . ."

Kate clutched her hands tightly in front of her. Why did she have to sacrifice her power?[32]

Because the battle lines are drawn so clearly in *Corporate Policy*, the resolution is hard to achieve, but when it comes, it brings Kate precisely what she wants: "Associated, marriage, a home, children. She was going to have it all." And she gets it. Returning to her office, she finds her secretary in a dither. Kate cannot come in yet; she is to go to Grant's office. There, she tells Grant "'I'm not some dolled-up piece of porcelain, and I don't want to be one. I'm an intelligent, capable woman, and I want to know what's going on downstairs . . . in my department.'" At last, he takes her downstairs where she finds the new sign on her door: "Kate Howard—President." They are, the hero promises, "a team"; she will be "'wife and business partner.'"[33]

32. Scott, *Corporate Policy*, pp. 218–19.
33. Ibid., pp. 206, 250.

The resolution of *Corporate Policy* appears to surrender romance entirely to the career woman, even to the woman who can articulate the vast and uncompromising range of her desires, the woman who wants it all. But there is a flaw in the perfection. When Kate refuses Grant's first marriage proposal, insisting on her right to her trust fund and stock, he sends her a letter firing her. He is the boss and she an employee. And it is as the boss that he promotes her; it is at his discretion and by his power that she is transformed into a president. Moreover, the story ends, like *Liberated Lady*, with a final note of sexuality, a nasty little double entendre. Kate, in her presidential office, begins to unbutton Grant's shirt, asking what they will do " 'after hours.' " " 'You'll be my wife,' " he replies, and Kate echoes, " 'Wife and business partner?' " " 'That's right, Kate,' he said, taking off her jacket and leading her to the sofa. 'And now, for starters, I suggest we get down to business.' " [34]

The career-woman heroine defies traditional romance mores by getting her man and keeping her career; in a number of these stories she defies those mores as well in accepting the hero as her lover early in the story. The consummation of sex does not, however, alter the romance formula. The heroine continues to be both aroused and frightened by her own sexuality, and the hero's sexual power over her continues to threaten her ability to maintain her selfhood, her will. Moreover, since no declaration of love accompanies these sexual acts, the heroine still comes slowly to the acknowledgment of her passion as the expression of her love, and must still wait in doubt for the hero to express his love for her.

What the consummated love scenes do affect, however, is the nature of the sexual conflict itself and, as a result, the larger area of gender conflict. The virginal heroine of traditional romance wages a battle against male power in the sexual arena. The newer heroine accepts sexuality more fully, both in her own erotic nature and, where fully developed love scenes occur, in her passional relationship with the hero. Sexuality is just as powerful a force as in more traditional romances, perhaps even more powerful, but it becomes less a source of conflict than a powerful new instrument for bonding hero and heroine. Passion may threaten to cloud the heroine's

34. Ibid., p. 250.

business judgment—and by the same token, the hero's—but it does not imperil her; it is no longer the hostile expression of male power and dominance. Male power does retain its potential threat, but it is now displaced, no longer an aspect of the hero but of the patriarchy proper, the father or the father-surrogate.

The career-woman heroine is presented as a character whose development has been blighted. She may, like Kate Howard in *Corporate Policy*, have accumulated an impressive array of successes, even successes traditionally associated with men, may be "Princeton, summa cum laude, Phi Beta Kappa. Yale Law School, law review, second in her class."[35] But Kate's intellectual growth has had its costs; emotionally, she remains a child. The element of sexual fantasy here, of course, is obvious, maintaining at least symbolically the virginal innocence of the heroine for the right man, for the hero who redeems her by making her a full woman. But the hero of contemporary romance has always been the initiator into womanhood as the source of sexual arousal and, ultimately, fulfillment for the heroine. What has changed is that the hero and his sexuality are purged of their negative aspects almost from the outset, and that the negative, alien, threatening elements of the patriarchy are displaced. The causes of the heroine's blight lie in her earlier life.

What these newer stories tell us, again and again, is that the source of the heroine's success and the source of her blighted self are the same. She inherits both her business and her lonely frigidity from her father or father-surrogate. The legacy of the Victorian father figure reappears in recent contemporary romance fiction, but it is a poisoned inheritance.

As a teenager, jealous of her father's second marriage, Kate Howard submerged her emotional life and concentrated on the studies she believed would win her his affection and respect: "Instead of dating, she had studied. She had gotten straight A's instead of corsages, been a member of the honor society instead of a cheerleader, valedictorian instead of prom queen—all to please her father, to make him proud of her and show him she was worthy of Associated." Kate hoped to inherit her father's business, but a broken

35. Ibid., p. 49.

engagement made him suspect that she was too weak; therefore, he placed her controlling shares in a trust fund. Betrayed by her father, Kate is wary of all men; nevertheless, she continues to hold herself to his criteria for success: competence, hard work, physical and emotional strength, above all ambition.

In Grant Brawley Kate finds a man who loves her, providing the affection she believed lost when her father remarried, and a man who respects her, providing the admiration she futilely sought from her father. In the resolution of the story, the hero is finally able to eradicate the betrayal of the father, making Kate the president of Associated Insurance as her father had promised. It is not a question in *Corporate Policy* of creating the hero in the image of the father. Kate sees immediately that, although Grant could be "warmly indulgent, almost paternal . . . he was much too young and virile to be any woman's father image."[36] The hero's function is to rescue the heroine from the malign influence of the father, not to replace him.[37]

36. Ibid., pp. 29, 16.

37. In some recent romances the malign paternal legacy is merely the function of accident, of events rather than character. This is the case in one version of the career-woman story that replaces the father with the surrogate of a much-older man the heroine loves and in some cases marries. In Ariel Berk's *Promise of Love*, Carla inherits her casting agency from her husband, who began it a few years before his death and, as he was dying, urged her to make it succeed. All romance heroes are older, but Alec was much older, in his fifties, old enough to be taken for Carla's father, even for her grandfather. His attitude toward her was always paternal: "To him she was 'Baby' or 'Kid,' the devoted young woman who delighted him simply by delighting in him, whose exuberance made him feel young." As a career woman and a widow, Carla suffers from her loss and from her failure, as yet unknown to her, to have achieved sexual fulfillment. The hero, of course, redeems her for sexual womanhood, and with him, in the veiled language of romance, Carla achieves her first orgasm. The hero's role, however, is not confined to the sexual sphere of the heroine's development; he is also charged with the responsibility of educating her into full, emotional, compassionate womanhood. The widowed heroine must learn to transfer her emotional loyalties, loyalties that are reduced at last merely to guilt. In *Promise of Love* the hero brings the heroine's life, intellectual and emotional, past and present, into harmonious fulfillment: "'Alec's been dead three years, Carla. . . . And you met me, and you fell in love'"; "'What you have to understand, Carla, is that you've got an incredible heart. It's got plenty of room for the present and the past. I'm not asking you to forget Alec. . . . if it weren't for him, you'd be a different person. And I wouldn't want you to be different. I want you just as you are" (pp. 36 and 184).

The motif of inheritance in recent romance stories of career wo-men appears with obsessive frequency,[38] for it provides a strategy by which romance writers can make their stories responsive to social change by allowing the heroine to enter and succeed in the market-place. Work has long been a necessity for the heroine of romance, but success in the marketplace threatens to defeminize her; ambition and womanliness are incompatible. The inheritance theme solves this dilemma, allowing the heroine to achieve high position without having to fight for it in the male world of business. But the inheri-tance theme, having apparently solved the problem of the career woman in romance, turns out in the hands of romance writers to carry the same penalties as independent success. The heroine con-tinues to suffer the erosion of her emotional potential, for these stories insist on tying the inheritance of the father's business to the legacy of loneliness, insecurity, and emotional frigidity.

The inheritance theme, finally, brings about a major adjustment in the subtext of aggression and revenge in romance fiction, for in the new corporate romances hostility toward the patriarchy is expressed as anger toward the father himself. To some degree that hostility can be seen as a reflex of the guilty uneasiness that accompanies the heroine's own economic success, especially since her success calls for no compensatory sacrifice. And by any measure the animus here is mild, marked more by regret than real anger. Nevertheless, it represents a profound change, particularly when compared with the Victorian romance in which the bestowal of the patrimony testifies to the loving benevolence of the father.

Such a metamorphosis in the father demonstrates how responsive romance fiction is to social change, or more accurately to changing perceptions of social conditions, no matter how slow such responses

---

38. The heroine of *The Fletcher Legacy* inherits her father's corporation along with an overwhelming sense of inadequacy in having failed to win his love. In *Passion's Prey* the heroine has become a biochemist, studying and working under an adored professor, "twenty-seven years her senior, long separated from his wife, the father of two children almost as old as she." At the opening of the story he has died, and the heroine is left to discover that she has stunted her own emotional and sexual growth through years of devotion to this father-surrogate (Ginger Chambers, *Passion's Prey* [Toronto: Harlequin Romances, 1984], p. 6).

may be in coming or how obliquely they are expressed. As a popular genre that rose and continues to flourish in response to bourgeois patriarchy, romance has always identified the antagonist with bourgeois power. The next chapter will explore further how romance has had continually to discover strategies for dealing with the fantasy acquisition of property, but it is already clear enough that contemporary romance has come totally to accept the bourgeois hero, the hero of the marketplace.

Unlike modern romance, Victorian romance located evil precisely in the active desire to acquire property. While the anachronistic feudal economy of these stories made it possible to ignore the marketplace specifically, a generalized notion of greedy ambition found full realization in the villain. The villain's single driving motivation was acquisition, whether sexual or economic. This was an important strategy because it separated the evil desire for acquisition from property itself. Property, in the form of hereditary estates, was thus rendered neutral or even good, something to be bestowed on one rather than struggled for. As long as romance could maintain this economic anachronism, the father could remain the expression of the patriarchy in its benign form.

Today feudal estates and aristocratic heroes are rare in romance; when fortunes are inherited, they are fortunes wrung from the arena of capitalism. As a result, the contemporary corporate heroine may, like her Victorian predecessor, inherit the patrimony, but she no longer has anyone on whom to avenge herself, not on the separate character of the villain and not on some aspect of villainy now elided into the figure of the hero. In that absence, she has no enemy left her but the very source of the patrimony itself.

5

THE EROTICS OF PROPERTY

"And of this place," thought she,
"I might have been mistress."

Jane Austen, *Pride and Prejudice*

$\mathscr{I}$t is a commonplace of romance that the heroine will marry well, a given that the hero will be rich. The heroine's accomplishment, moreover, her success in marrying well, must seem almost an accident; it is never her purpose. The idea of a romance heroine setting out to marry successfully is doubly denied. She never seeks marriage in any form, and when she finds her hero, she is never drawn to him by the signs of his economic power. The heroine is defined by her apparent passivity and disinterestedness; she is a negation of the purposeful, self-interested, mercenary woman. Because she seeks nothing, she finds everything, and her innocent progress from rags to riches has been a familiar route since Samuel Richardson's *Pamela*. The heroine's chastity and her economic disinterestedness have been maintained with equal care for over two-and-a-half centuries.[1]

Romance fiction offers a fantasy of female success, specifically economic success, the aggressive nature of which it thoroughly masks under the heroine's extreme economic innocence. Economically passive, the conventional romance heroine displaces her energy into the approved and unthreatening activity of preserving her virginity. This strategy, basic to the romance formula, attempts to disguise both the heroine's real goal and the profound association between sexual and economic power that lies at the heart of romance, as realized in the figure of the romance hero. Economic success becomes a condition of the hero of romance. It is not simply a matter of the hero's wealth as an added-on value; his wealth, his property and economic power, are basic attributes of his masculinity, a principal source of his virile attractiveness. The roots of this configuration of

---

1. In her discussion of Harlequin romances, Tania Modleski notes that the problem of getting "your heroine from loneliness and penury to romance and riches, without making her appear to have helped herself along or even to have thought about the matter, is an old problem for novelists" (*Loving with a Vengeance* [Hamden, Conn.: Archon Books, 1982], pp. 48–49); and see Robert Palfrey Utter and Gwendolyn Bridges Needham, *Pamela's Daughters* (New York: Russell and Russell, 1936).

the romance hero lie in the structures of bourgeois and patriarchal society, in the condition of women, and in the fictional strategies devised over nearly two centuries to provide women a rich amalgam of conventional wisdom and fantasy gratification.

This chapter investigates the sources of the contemporary romance hero as a sign of male economic power and of the union of sexual and economic energy. Certainly, the fact that sexual and economic energy have become inextricably linked points to the degree to which women have understood them as male sources of power and male symbols of power—the very types of power from which women have been excluded. At the heart of this complex of values is the exclusion of women from economic power, especially the increasing isolation of women from the sources of money that came with the hegemony of the bourgeoisie at the end of the eighteenth and the beginning of the nineteenth century.

The conditions of bourgeois society rendered women economically powerless; they were excluded not only from participation in the bourgeois marketplace but from the principal myth of bourgeois society, the myth of upward mobility. Young men, so the myth promised, could rise through their own initiative and industry. No such promise was held out to young women. Women could not rise by their own efforts; moreover, individual initiative in even a generalized sense was negatively sanctioned. Modesty and passivity became the conventionally valued characteristics of women, characteristics that guaranteed the absence of the aggressive self-seeking that bourgeois society rewarded.

Women's only means for rising socially and economically was marriage, but marrying for reasons of money and status lost respectability during these years. This represented, of course, a revolutionary change from marriage conventions in feudal society. Though it is fatuous to idealize the condition of women under feudalism, it is still useful to recognize that when property consisted primarily of land, and marriages were arranged to consolidate real property and power, women were placed in a far less ambiguous position than in bourgeois society.

With the rise of the bourgeoisie, as the traditional basis of marriage in family and property came into conflict with the ideal of romantic love, a deep disdain developed for marriage based on economic considerations. It is perhaps the most extravagant irony in the history of women that romantic love, with its source in the celebration of woman in chivalric romance, should have become a means for exacerbating the powerlessness of women. To that end, much in the tradition of courtly love was inverted, most significantly the power relations between lovers.

Courtly love celebrated a mistress married to a lord more powerful than the youthful, aspiring suitor. By virtue of her marriage the desired lady was socially and economically superior to her lover, perhaps older as well. The lover aspired above his station, but the expressed object of his desire was not the property or status of the beloved, but her person. Love alone motivated him. To the extent that courtly love literature answered the needs of men, it did so by constructing a compensatory fantasy for those young bachelors who remained wifeless precisely because they were propertyless.[2] The adulterous base of courtly love not only set it apart from the marriage relationship, with its basis in property, but served to deny property altogether as an element of desire. Thus, in this fantasy, love, precisely because it was altogether distinct from property relations, became "the centre of man's life."[3] In his extravagant valuation of love and in his complete disinterest in property, the courtly lover prefigured the heroine of modern romance.

Bourgeois society eventually adopted a version of romantic love, one corrupted into a respectability suitable to the new middle classes. Now, power, in the form of property and station, as well as superior age, became attributes of the desired male, and if modest bourgeois women never actually pressed their own romantic suits, the implication remained that in marriage it was the woman who

2. Shulamith Shahar cites Rene Nelli (*Lumiere du Graal*, 1951), who notes that "the ideal of love between a married woman and a young bachelor fitted in with the aspirations of the young wandering knight, those *juvenes* many of whom were bachelors only for lack of choice, because they had no property" (*The Fourth Estate: A History of Women in the Middle Ages*, trans. Chaya Galai [New York: Methuen, 1983], p. 165).

3. Shulamith Shahar argues that "love in courtly literature is the centre of man's life," and that this conception stands "in complete contrast both to the marriage customs of the nobility . . . and to the status of the married woman" (ibid., p. 161).

had everything to gain. But ambiguities increased with the complex social and economic changes of the late eighteenth century. New fortunes challenged established forms of status and power; land and money intermarried, confusing traditional class distinctions and confounding traditional marriage expectations.[4]

Hand in hand with the shift in economic power from a landed aristocracy to an entrepreneurial bourgeoisie went the spread of the ideal of romantic love as the basis for marriage. It was precisely the interplay between these two forces that accomplished the complete alienation of women from the dominant values of their society. Enjoined from participation in the marketplace, they were denied the expression of ambition and individualism. In a dramatically parallel way, the application of the new values of romantic love to marriage, now conceived as a romantic rather than an economic alliance, denied women their only remaining opportunity for economic self-improvement. The courtship period, moreover, reinforced the necessity for women to represent themselves as modest, passive, and submissive—the inverse of those aspects of character that promised men personal success.

The victory of romantic love over economic considerations as a basis for marriage was not won overnight. The uncertainties and disruptions of flux and change as the feudal order was displaced by bourgeois capitalism were echoed in the ambiguities investing ideas and values about marriage. According to Lawrence Stone, "It was only in the eighteenth century that there appeared signs of a new upper-class ideal, to channel sexual desire into the marriage bond and keep it there." But even as that ideal took root, the older view of marriage remained the common one, and that view distrusted love, or lust, "as a secure basis for marriage." But by the end of

4. Mary Poovey points to the "increasingly anomalous" position of women as "competition and confrontation replaced the old paternalistic alliances of responsibilities and dependences," which had "in some very practical ways" protected women. The new social construction of gender "idealized [women's] helplessness" and isolated them in the domestic sphere; in that way the ideal of womanhood was "increasingly at odds with the competitive spirit that was rapidly transfiguring every other sector of English society" (*The Proper Lady and the Woman Writer: Ideology as Style in the Works of Mary Wollstonecraft, Mary Shelley, and Jane Austen* [Chicago: University of Chicago Press, 1984], pp. xv–xvi).

the eighteenth century romantic love was winning out, and according to Stone, after 1780, "for the first time in history, romantic love became a respectable motive for marriage among the propertied classes." Basic to the ideal of romantic love is that "love is the most important thing in the world, to which all other considerations, *particularly material ones*, should be sacrificed" (emphasis mine).[5]

Romance fiction arose as a response to the situation of women, doubly enjoined against seeking their own economic success: first by the strictures of bourgeois society in relation to work and the marketplace, and second by the values of romantic love as they affected marriage. These strictures were not, of course, independent of each other; they worked together to consolidate male power by enlisting romantic love itself as an ideology of the patriarchy. Marriage became the locus of the essential contradiction for women in regard to property and to romantic love. It is precisely in response to this contradiction that romance fiction was born, a genre that in its surface story appears to accept the conditions imposed on women by society and to start from the premises of bourgeois culture in regard to women. The fantasy gratification provided by romance comes through the achievement of the heroine's success in marrying well in spite of those conditions. The particular brilliance of romance fiction is the way it covers its own tracks in the interests of serving both convention and fantasy; for the central, the elemental, condition that romance honors in the surface text is the economic disinterestedness of the heroine.

In *The Family, Sex and Marriage*, Lawrence Stone isolates three ideas about marriage in order to make the point that these are not universal beliefs but "modern Western culture-bound preconceptions." The first of these preconceptions is central to romance fiction: "that there is a clear dichotomy between marriage for interest,

5. Lawrence Stone, *The Family, Sex and Marriage in England 1500–1800* (New York: Harper and Row, 1977), pp. 282, 284. Philippe Aries presents the same view, if somewhat cynically. After the eighteenth century, he says, "The west gradually adopted an ideal of marriage requiring husband and wife to love each other (or appear to), like real lovers. Extra-conjugal erotics found their way into the marriage bed" (Philippe Aries and Andre Bejin, ed. *Western Sexuality: Practice and Precept in Past and Present Times*, trans. Anthony Forster [London: Basil Blackwell, 1986], p. 137).

meaning money, status or power, and marriage for affect, meaning love, friendship or sexual attraction; and that the first is morally reprehensible."[6] To be sure, not only romance, but Anglo-American fiction of all types during the past two centuries respects this notion, and men as well as women are enjoined from marrying for money. However, romance fiction alone has found the strategies to free women from the cultural immobility enforced on them. Though these strategies have altered over time, they are unvarying in their apparent loyalty to the belief that marriage for interest is "morally reprehensible," insisting on marrying the heroine "for affect" alone, but marrying her to a man with "money, status [and] power."

The basic strategy of romance fiction can be seen in its most elemental form in Richardson's *Pamela*, a story that, in its essentials, lies at the heart of contemporary romance: the preservation of virginity rewarded by marriage to a wealthy man. Beyond that elemental pattern, however, *Pamela* does not bring us far in understanding the more complex tactics of romance or the development of the romance hero as a sign of economic power. Richardson's novel is both too extreme a fantasy and too little engaged in disguising the vulgar barter of virginity for property. The extent of the socioeconomic fantasy in *Pamela* exceeds the limits permitted even in a genre dedicated to fantasy gratification. In allowing chastity-preserved to leap the vast social gulf between servant girl and aristocrat, Richardson undercuts, even derides, the story he tells. Moreover, since Pamela as a character is virtually reduced to the repository of chastity, she has nothing to offer in marriage but her physical person—attractive and intact.

The excess and the vulgarity of *Pamela*, elements that undercut its effectiveness as fantasy, may have their source in Richardson himself, for male authors are anomalous in romance fiction.[7] The assertion that woman's fantasy cannot be created by male writers

6. Stone, *The Family, Sex and Marriage*, p. 86.
7. The romance readers Janice Radway studies claim they can tell when a romance has been written by a man, that such "a man's story always gives the hero's point of view more extensively than that of the heroine" (*Reading the Romance: Women, Patriarchy and Popular Culture* [Chapel Hill: University of North Carolina Press, 1984], pp. 179–80).

is an uncomfortable one, but if, in fact, the ritual, formulaic material of romance comes from women's psychological response to their situation within a bourgeois and patriarchal society, then it is not unlikely that the fantasy material forged by that situation would be inaccessible to men. Moreover, Richardson's choice of the epistolary form for *Pamela*, though it may provide a woman's "voice," does violence to the necessarily innocent unself-consciousness of the romance heroine. Tania Modleski makes this important point in her analysis of narrative point of view in *Pamela* by showing that the epistolary form requires that the heroine be self-consciously aware of her own charms and their effect on Lord B.: "in order to tell her own story, she came to possess the very knowledge she should never have acquired."[8]

The significant source for the strategies of romance and for the establishment of the romance hero whose economic power is intrinsic to his appeal is not Richardson's *Pamela* but Jane Austen's *Pride and Prejudice*. Jane Austen's Darcy, like Richardson's Lord B., is rich and aristocratic; but in *Pride and Prejudice*, Darcy's wealth and station are not merely the source of his superiority to the heroine but additionally the source of his masculine attraction. Austen's heroine, like the romance heroines who follow, is granted the fantasy happy ending that combines, in Stone's terms, "interest" and "affect," but unlike the heroines of romance, Elizabeth Bennet is not kept innocent of the economic advantages Darcy offers. Austen does not keep her heroine's eyes modestly averted from the hero's wealth and station. On the contrary, Elizabeth's eyes open wide when she sees the visible sign of wealth and station, when she sees Darcy's property and feels "that to be mistress of Pemberley might be something!"[9] The happy ending of *Pride and Prejudice*, with Elizabeth's rise to wealth and station as "mistress of Pemberley" is a fantasy resolution, but fantasy based on a clear-eyed understanding of the advantages of marriage for interest.

Austen's treatment of economic conditions extends beyond her

8. Modleski, *Loving with a Vengeance*, p. 54.

9. Jane Austen, *Pride and Prejudice*, ed. Donald J. Gray (1813; New York: W. W. Norton, 1966), p. 167.

acknowledgment of marriage for interest. *Pride and Prejudice* reflects the changing and unsettled economic world of the late-eighteenth and early-nineteenth centuries in the disposition of its male characters along a socioeconomic spectrum.[10] Darcy, with his inherited property, represents a precapitalist stability of class and wealth. The situation of the other male characters belies that stability, from Mr. Bennet with his five daughters and his property entailed in the male line, to Bingley, only now establishing himself as gentry on the inherited proceeds of his father's business. The Gardiners, Elizabeth's aunt and uncle, are in trade, a condition that Austen refuses to treat with conventional snobbery, just as she refuses to accord conventional respect to the traditional professions. In *Pride and Prejudice*, the professions are exemplified in Mr. Collins the clergyman and Wickham the soldier, respectively a fool and a knave.

The eligible bachelors in *Pride and Prejudice* represent a microcosm of the available choices open to Elizabeth and her sisters and friends. They include landed gentry with aristocratic connections, the new gentry recently elevated beyond trade, and the professions. Despite the dignity accorded the Gardiners, it is worth noting that there are no suitors in this novel who are in trade. Thus, Austen sketches here the general range of acceptable suitors for genteel

10. Ellen Moers provides a fine analysis of the class structure and distribution of wealth in *Pride and Prejudice*, and she points out the great importance of money in all of Austen's novels, particularly the importance of money to marriage: "Marriage makes money a serious business in Austen's fiction; her seriousness about money makes marriage important, as in fact it was in the England of her day." In the context of money and class, Moers brings particular emphasis to the point that Darcy is an "improbable close friend for such as Bingley, and an even less probable catch for Elizabeth Bennet" (*Literary Women* [New York: Doubleday, 1976], pp. 67, 69).

Northrop Frye also points out that the marriages that mark the happy endings of Jane Austen's novels are made to seem believable despite their being, in fact, highly unlikely: "If we concentrate on the shape of [Austen's] stories, we are studying something that brings her much closer to her romantic colleagues, even to the writers of the horrid mysteries she parodied. Her characters are believable, yet every so often we become aware of the tension between them and the outlines of the story into which they are obliged to fit. This is particularly true of the endings, where the right men get married to the right women, although the inherent unlikelihood of these unions has been the main theme of the story" (*The Secular Scripture: A Study of the Structure of Romance* [Cambridge: Harvard University Press, 1976], pp. 39–40).

girls, and it is a fairly narrow range. Moreover, the choices narrow even more drastically; as the novel works its way through proposals, elopements, and marriages, only the gentry, established or new, is shown as the source of any really desirable mates. When one counts the number of marriageable girls and women in *Pride and Prejudice*— the five Bennet sisters, Charlotte Lucas, Georgina Darcy, Anne de Bourgh, and Miss Bingley—the seriousness of the marriage problem becomes even clearer. Good, bad, or indifferent, there are simply too few bachelors to go around.

With so clear-eyed a view of the marriage situation, it is little wonder that Jane Austen mocks the Gothic romances of her time, romances that so thoroughly displaced the real problems inherent in marrying, with their source in the new configurations of the economic order, the emerging power of money and its challenge to inherited real property, and the consequences of these changes for altering the value not only of marriageable men but of marriageable women as well. Elizabeth is a perfect example. She is gentry, her father a landed gentleman. But, with all due irony, the male entail on the property deprives Elizabeth of at least some degree of her status, and therefore her value, which in turn reduces her marketability. And without any significant wealth, without, that is, the new source of value in a rising bourgeoisie, Elizabeth falls between the old and the new, a victim of the change from a feudal to a market society. She is not, as the French put it, a *parti*.

In the face of such dilemmas the sexual threat of the Gothic villain pales; he might have the power to cause a psychosexual frisson, but none whatever to pose a realistic threat. The sexual threat, for Austen, lies in a much more probable villain, a charming soldier, an apparent gentleman. It is not a question of fending off sexual attack but of guarding oneself against romantic or sexual appeal, against what Stone calls "affect," for such an appeal could be strong enough to make one disregard entirely the economic side of marriage, or what Stone calls "interest."

Mr. Collins and Wickham stand for interest and affect as disjunct and isolated motives for marriage not only in their unions with Charlotte and Lydia, but also as rival suitors for Elizabeth. Because Mr. Collins is a comic character and because Elizabeth never takes his marriage proposal seriously, it might seem possible to dismiss him as playing no significant part in the structure of the novel as it unfolds the story of Elizabeth's education for marriage. Moreover, because Elizabeth is for a time attracted to Wickham, it might appear that *Pride and Prejudice* works through what would become the conventional opposition of two male figures, hero and villain, the good Darcy versus the evil Wickham.[11] In fact, the structure of Austen's novel is not established on a polarity between Wickham and Darcy, but on the exemplary opposition between Wickham and Mr. Collins, two suitors, both wrong but for different reasons, and on the resolution of that opposition through Darcy.

Mr. Collins, pompous and stupid as he is, as much of a toady to Lady Catherine as he may be, must be taken seriously as the representation of marriage for interest in *Pride and Prejudice*. It is Mr. Collins, after all, who is prepared to rescue the Bennet sisters from the threatened loss of their home, and Mr. Collins whom Charlotte accepts, despite all his personal shortcomings, because she understands that marriage is "the only honourable provision for well-educated women of small fortune, and however uncertain of giving happiness, must be their pleasantest preservative from want."[12] In other words, Mr. Collins offers nothing but an appeal to interest; there is no other imaginable reason for marrying him.

To be sure, Austen is very shrewd in how she uses Mr. Collins. For one thing, the whole Collins episode serves as something of a blind, for it is of course Darcy who offers real money and status. Moreover, the very fact that Mr. Collins is a comic figure makes the appeal of interest much weaker for Elizabeth; when interest comes

---

11. Jean Kennard sees the two-suitor convention in fiction as "firmly established" by Jane Austen and points out that an Austen heroine's maturity comes with her choice of the right suitor over the wrong one, who "embodies the qualities [the heroine] must reject" (*Victims of Convention* [Hamden, Conn.: Archon Books, 1978], p. 11). Insofar as Wickham and Darcy represent the opposition of good and evil qualities between which Elizabeth must learn to discriminate, Kennard's analysis is a useful way of understanding the changes in Elizabeth's character that mark her achievement of maturity. But Wickham's attraction for Elizabeth and the consequent conflict between the right and the wrong suitor are fairly short lived, ending with Darcy's long explanatory letter and preceding Elizabeth's visit to Pemberley.

12. Austen, *Pride and Prejudice*, p. 86.

in the person of Mr. Collins, it is hardly a temptation at all, at least for the heroine. But Charlotte Lucas is not the Other Woman of romance fiction and in allowing her to accept Mr. Collins, Austen is much clearer eyed than the romance writers who follow her; in Austen's world a woman need not be evil to marry for money.

Marriage for affect, however, causes much greater misery in Austen's world than marriage for interest. In *Pride and Prejudice* it is folly to undertake the serious business of marriage for emotional considerations alone, whether these are called affection, love, passion, fancy, or the "captivat[ion] by youth and beauty, and that appearance of good humour, which youth and beauty generally give," this last describing the short-term allure that brought Mr. Bennet his long-term marriage with his foolish and ignorant wife.[13]

Through the character of Wickham, Austen dramatizes the dangers of affect. Elizabeth herself is attracted to Wickham despite the fact that his poverty makes him ineligible as a suitor. The degree to which Elizabeth's celebrated good sense is in abeyance in her relationship to Wickham is emphasized by her willingness to accept his false report of Darcy's behavior as the truth. But it is in Wickham's elopement with Lydia that Austen most emphatically demonstrates the dangers of affect. Attracted to the handsome soldier and urged on by vanity and folly, Lydia lacks any protective self-interest whatsoever. Not only does she fail to assure herself that the man she marries can support her; she fails to assure herself that the man she runs off with will marry her at all.

The whole point of *Pride and Prejudice* is that Elizabeth will succeed where both Charlotte and Lydia fail. But Austen is extremely canny in establishing Elizabeth's character, taking considerable pains to make it clear that her heroine is, at the outset, more likely to succumb to affect than to interest. Since Elizabeth's marriage will be a triumph of upward mobility, it is essential to absolve her of innate self-interest. For that reason, it is crucial to the moral structure of *Pride and Prejudice* that she be attracted to Wickham, a personable young man whose only apparent fault is his poverty. In overlooking his poverty, Elizabeth offers proof of her disinterestedness and,

13. Ibid., p. 162.

consequently, of the greater danger, for her, of allowing affect alone to guide her.

Having established Elizabeth's credentials as a disinterested heroine, and concomitantly downplaying interest as a serious motive for her, Austen begins to shift the balance between interest and affect. When Wickham's villainy is uncovered, we discover that his poverty is not an accidental characteristic; he has incurred poverty through his viciousness of character. Wickham is not poor but honest, but poor and vicious—even poor *because* he is vicious. And in the absence of any poor but honest suitors in this Austen novel to offset Wickham's character, an oblique connection is forged between poverty—at least in suitors—and vicious habits.

The economic instability of Austen's world is echoed in the shifting values accorded to marriages made on traditional terms of interest or on the more radical basis of affect. The care with which Austen absolves Elizabeth of economic self-seeking suggests that a girl who marries well might find herself the subject of cynical gossip. And the careful strategies in *Pride and Prejudice* also tell us that while marriage for interest might be considered the greater social crime for women, marriage for affect alone brings considerably heavier penalties. Elizabeth is made to walk a very narrow path before she is rewarded with the happy ending of romance. Like all romance heroines after her, she marries happily and marries well but, uniquely, Elizabeth does so only after she recognizes and acknowledges the complicity of property in the masculine allure of the hero.

Pemberley is the sign of Darcy's social and economic power and it is there that Elizabeth comes to see Darcy in a new light. By this point in the novel, Elizabeth has rejected both marriage for interest and marriage for affect, and with that stage of her education complete, she is ready to encounter Pemberley.

With her Aunt and Uncle Gardiner, her relatives "in trade," Elizabeth approaches Darcy's house through his woods and park, and when at last Pemberley House comes into view, "she felt, that to be mistress of Pemberley might be something!" As the housekeeper shows them through the house, Elizabeth repeats this idea, now with regret: "'And of this place . . . I might have been mistress!'"

The housekeeper, moreover, speaks nothing but Darcy's praise: he is "handsome," "good-tempered," "generous-hearted," "affable to the poor," "the best landlord and master that ever lived," and to her mind, not proud. Elizabeth begins to feel "a more gentle sensation" toward Darcy at this catalogue of his virtues, and she becomes newly aware of Darcy as a man of responsibilities and of power: "As a brother, a landlord, a master, she considered how many people's happiness were in his guardianship!—How much of pleasure or pain it was his to bestow!—How much of good or evil must be done by him!"[14] When at last Darcy himself appears, a host all kindness to Elizabeth and all civility to the Gardiners, Elizabeth comes to recognize her new feelings for Darcy, feelings of respect and esteem, and of gratitude to him for loving her.

Throughout this central episode in *Pride and Prejudice*, Pemberley House stands as the powerful emblem of Darcy's wealth and station, of his economic allure. It is even possible to see Darcy and Pemberley as one, as merely two different material expressions of the same elegance, taste, beauty, and power of rank. Austen makes us recognize that Elizabeth feels the appeal of such power, the appeal of being "mistress of Pemberley." Through the symbol of Darcy's house, *Pride and Prejudice* establishes the erotics of property.

Austen makes this point once again, long after the Pemberley scene, when Elizabeth confesses to Jane, in her comical, teasing way, that she is to marry Darcy. Jane is incredulous and curious; begging Elizabeth to be serious, she asks that she tell her everything: "'Will you tell me how long you have loved him?'" Elizabeth is not quite prepared to be serious: "'It has been coming on so gradually, that I hardly know when it began. But I believe I must date it from my first seeing his beautiful grounds at Pemberley.'" Jane, of course, is hardly satisfied. "Another intreaty that [Elizabeth] would be serious, however, produced the desired effect; and she soon satisfied Jane by her solemn assurances of attachment."[15] Yet we hear none of Elizabeth's solemn recital; we are left with the union of love and property, whatever Austen's irony.

14. Ibid., pp. 167–71.
15. Ibid., p. 258.

The marriage of Elizabeth and Darcy is a marriage between equals, Darcy's social and economic superiority notwithstanding. Like other elements of *Pride and Prejudice*, the personal equality finally achieved by the hero and heroine is borrowed by romance fiction. And in romance fiction, as in *Pride and Prejudice*, the conditions on which this equality rests are problematic. Obviously, it cannot be based on socioeconomic status, since it is a condition of the hero that he be socially and economically superior to the heroine and that he will bestow rank and fortune on her. Therefore, Elizabeth, like the romance heroine after her, must offer something different as her part of the bargain. In fact, she offers a kind of moral tutelage, and in this solution to the problem of equality Austen turns to the newly developing conception of woman. Denied power, she has been compensated with virtue, and even the far-from-conventional Elizabeth is woman enough to serve as a moral mentor. Certainly the belief that a fair bargain has been struck between two parties when one offers rank and wealth and the other, moral improvement is the kind of pious wish-fulfillment called on to mask social relations that are far less benign, the kind of wish-fulfillment, moreover, that is expressed most satisfactorily within the closed structures of fiction. But this convention, however disingenuous, is essential for Austen and for romance writers, for they must not only assure their heroines' economic security but establish them as well in a marriage based on an equilibrium of personal power between husband and wife.

The question of equilibrium is central to romance fiction, for it alone promises the heroine a happy married future. Given the socioeconomic disparity between hero and heroine, a necessary condition of the story as a fantasy of upward mobility, there are only two ways in which equilibrium can be achieved: either the heroine must rise to the hero's station, or the hero must fall from his eminence. In *Pride and Prejudice*, however, equilibrium is achieved without violent changes in the social or sexual roles of the hero or heroine. Elizabeth's ability to offer Darcy moral tutelage invests her with moral superiority tantamount to his social and economic superiority. Moreover, the success of the heroine in improving the character of the hero is not only a tribute to her as a moral exemplar but a tribute as well to the hero, already near enough to perfection to require no ruder means of correction. No fall from eminence is necessary in Darcy's case; the sacrifice of his pride suffices, his willingness to love not only Elizabeth but even her relatives in trade. Darcy learns his moral lesson; there is no concomitant vitiation of his physical or economic power.

The equilibrium Austen achieved in *Pride and Prejudice* represents a twofold victory for fantasy, for the power of fiction to correct what real social conditions have set awry. The first part of that achievement is simply to have made credible a marriage that bridges the considerable social distance between Elizabeth and Darcy. The second, and the more remarkable, achievement is to have created an equilibrium between the lovers at a time when the conditions affecting marriage, particularly for the gentry, were more complex and ambiguous than at any later period. Both the appearance of newly moneyed men as viable suitors and the confusion between competing values of interest and affect contribute to the problem. But before long, both the bourgeois suitor and romantic love become commonplace with the paradoxical effect that marriage for interest is at one and the same time accepted in the person of the suitor and denied in the convention of romantic love.

As a result, the benign equilibrium effected by Jane Austen cannot last, for while romance writers borrow her resolution in equilibrium and continue to invest moral superiority in the heroine, they no longer accept moral tutelage as an adequate means of achieving that equilibrium. By the time of Charlotte Brontë's *Jane Eyre* much more violent means are necessary to make the heroine the hero's equal, and what is of particular importance here is that violence is done not only to the person of the hero, in the loss of Rochester's hand and sight, but also to the property of the hero. Thornfield is Rochester's home and as such it is the emblem of his power as a property owner, a power made doubly significant by Jane's first relationship to him as a paid employee in that house. In the destruction of Thornfield, Brontë creates a symbol for the termination of Rochester's social and economic superiority to Jane. And in the destruction of Thornfield by Bertha, Brontë makes a woman responsible for Rochester's symbolic fall from power. Jane, of course, cannot carry out that act herself, cannot herself do violence to Rochester and his power. Jane's innocence of such a wish is proven well in advance when she thwarts Bertha's earlier attempt at arson. Nevertheless, whatever the displacement of aggression onto Bertha, the fact remains that Thornfield is destroyed by a woman's hand.

Elizabeth Bennet marries Darcy and lives as mistress of Pemberley. It is unimaginable that Jane Austen would find it necessary to destroy Darcy's ancestral home, for in doing so she would fatally diminish Darcy's value as well as Elizabeth's own future happiness. In thinking about Brontë's destruction of Thornfield, it is worth giving our attention not only to the way in which it diminishes Rochester but to the limits it sets on Jane Eyre's own rise to economic power.

Appropriately, Jane's reunion with Rochester comes not at Thornfield but at Ferndean, and Ferndean is no ancestral manor.

> The manor-house of Ferndean was a building of considerable antiquity, moderate size, and no architectural pretensions, deep buried in a wood. . . . [Mr. Rochester's] father had purchased the estate for the sake of the game covers. He would have let the house: but could find no tenants, in consequence of its ineligible and insalubrious site. Ferndean then remained unfurnished; with the exception of some two or three rooms fitted up for the accommodation of the squire when he went there in the season to shoot.[16]

Jane marries Rochester, but she does not become mistress of Thornfield. In thus reducing the hero's power, Brontë has imposed considerable restrictions on the extent of the heroine's socioeconomic achievement. After *Pride and Prejudice*, the equilibrium established between the hero and the heroine comes at a significant cost, a cost directly borne by the hero but indirectly suffered by the heroine. The statement this strategy makes is twofold. First, it asserts the vulnerability of the hero in all his arrogance of male, patriarchal power; and in that way it serves the aggressive subtext of vengeance that moves through romance fiction. But second, it limits the success

16. Charlotte Brontë, *Jane Eyre* (New York: Random House, 1943), p. 326.

of the heroine; and in that way argues, after the fact, for her economic disinterestedness, thereby reinforcing the conventional values of marriage for love alone.

The romance hero, his personal value signified by his wealth and status, has his source in Darcy and undergoes his primary modification in Rochester, a modification dramatized by the survival of Pemberley and the destruction of Thornfield. In this metamorphosis of the hero from Darcy to Rochester lie critically important clues to the development of the contemporary romance hero. In Darcy, Austen brings together elements that romance writers subsequently find disconcertingly inextricable, if no longer invulnerable. Darcy is at once good-looking, a "fine, tall person, handsome features, noble mien,"[17] and the aristocrat of the novel, allied to nobility through his mother, the heir of a fine property from his father, with an income of ten thousand pounds a year, all this signified by Pemberley. In Rochester, Brontë adds the element of overt sexuality, and with that sexuality the dark hero of romance becomes not simply a man with a moral flaw but a potential source of danger and terror. Though masculine power remains a union of physical and economic allure in this hero, it is now specifically signified through sexual power, which, in conjunction with economic power, charges the hero with a new and threatening potency. Sexuality and property become the signs of the hero, so deeply and mutually implicated in one another that each might stand as a metaphor for the other. Brontë shows us this, again, in the maiming of Rochester and particularly in the destruction of Thornfield, accomplishing both the real loss of property and the symbolic attack on sexuality. The complicity of sexual and economic power is made patently clear in the narrative of Thornfield's final destruction, when Brontë insists on repeating the history of the earlier fire in which Bertha's attack on both husband and property is specifically sexual, for she " 'nearly burnt her husband in his bed.' "[18]

The Victorian romance writers inherit the fusion of sexual and economic energy in the figure of the dark hero, but in their hands

17. Austen, *Pride and Prejudice*, p. 6.
18. Brontë, *Jane Eyre*, p. 324.

the elements of sexual power and economic power are rearranged and distorted in a denial of both marketplace economics and male sexual power. The Victorians are not the first to ignore the marketplace, of course. Even Jane Austen, with her realistic reflection of the economic changes her society was undergoing, chooses her hero Darcy from the landed gentry and makes his wealth inherited, ancestral property passed down the patriarchal generations. And though Charlotte Brontë exposes her heroine to the necessities of earning a living, her hero, too, is isolated from bourgeois money making. Rochester, of course, loses his patriarchal home and inheritance, and is reduced to living in a manorhouse purchased only a generation earlier. Still, he is not sent into the marketplace. But by the second half of the nineteenth century, and especially in novels written in America, the establishment of ancestral homes and great inheritances had become altogether anachronistic.

For popular Victorian romance writers like May Agnes Fleming and Harriet Lewis the value of recreating the economic system of feudal society is twofold. First, they can alter the nature of the hero, at once purifying and vitiating him: by keeping him out of the marketplace, they protect his economic innocence; and by withholding property they reduce his masculine power. Second, they can keep property altogether out of the hands of any male character of marriageable age, either hero or villain, as long as it remains in a sort of fantasy escrow, in the keeping of the elderly father-surrogate. Thus property is always in doubt in these romances and as long as property is withheld, the male figure cannot realize his full potency. Conversely, in both Austen and Brontë, the heroes' fathers have long been dead and the heroes, from the time we meet them, are fully in command of their property and their concomitant power.

Since property is withheld in Victorian romance, kept, that is, in the hands of the father, neither villain nor hero can stand as an expression of economic power. In place of economic power, Lewis and Fleming create what can best be called economic energy, the drive for power, the lusting after inherited wealth, and confer that energy on the villain, thereby effecting a profound change in the dynamics of romance fiction. Their stories make such economic energy in the hands of men so alien from women and so threatening to them that marriage as a union with those who wield it becomes unthinkable. As a result male power is no longer presented as something women can acquire through marriage, through love. So great is the ambivalence of the Victorian romance writer toward economic power that the storyline allows the heroine to act simultaneously as the serene recipient of property bestowed on her by the benevolent father, *and* as the active appropriator of property violently torn from the clutches of the villain.

Violence, however, is readily available to the Victorian heroine. With sexual and economic energy invested in the character of the villain, it is no longer necessary to limit or half-disguise the violence done to a powerful male figure; it can be altogether unleashed, the villain utterly destroyed—discovered, disinherited, finally dead. Not only is this violence permissible because the villain now stands as the locus of power, but it is available to the heroine at no cost to herself. Because she destroys the villain as the symbol of male power and not the hero, the heroine herself does not suffer from the fall he undergoes; her personal ambitions can still be completely fulfilled. Destroying the villain, appropriating the inheritance, and capping her economic success with the requisite, but entirely insignificant, marriage to the sexually and economically innocent hero, the Victorian heroine succeeds.

The solution to the economic powerlessness of women afforded by Victorian romance is an escape into a fantasy of total power, but a fantasy that altogether surrenders romantic love as a goal. In Lawrence Stone's terms, interest entirely overwhelms affect, not specifically as a motive for marriage but as a fantasy of female fulfillment. But the strategies adopted by Lewis and Fleming cannot last; the fatal diminution of the hero, and consequently of romantic love, is too extreme to survive the new construction of female sexuality that develops in our century. Romance fiction has to resurrect the value of affect.

The new strategies through which romance fiction redeems the hero and with him the power of love have their source in *Gone with the Wind*, for Margaret Mitchell discovers a way to return the fused elements of economic and sexual power to the character of the hero. In the calculated shift of hero status from Ashley Wilkes to

Rhett Butler, Mitchell finally rescues romance from the economics of feudal society and firmly establishes her hero's power within the capitalist marketplace. The profound effect of Mitchell's economic realism is that it reinstates the hero as the center of male power in romance.

In *Jane Eyre* Charlotte Brontë reverses the characteristics of hero and villain and leaves Victorian romance writers with the electric legacy of Rochester. But Rochester, for writers like Harriet Lewis and May Agnes Fleming, is too overtly an expression of male sexual power, and they return him to the role of villain, while the hero, still cut in the mold of St. John Rivers, becomes a weak and sexless character. In the early chapters of *Gone with the Wind* Mitchell returns to the conventional pre-Brontë images of hero and villain, but, in the course of the novel, she transfers hero status from the fair aristocrat to the dark and brooding, sensual man.

When *Gone with the Wind* opens, we see, if only in its final hours, the antebellum South, a precapitalist society, virtually a feudal society. For that brief period, Ashley—the undisputed heir of Twelve Oaks—is easily identified as the true hero of romance. Son of the master of Twelve Oaks, he belongs to the leading family in the county; he is the novel's aristocrat. He is first described as riding up to Tara, "his drowsy gray eyes wide with a smile and the sun so bright on his blond hair that it seemed like a cap of shining silver." Educated, cultivated, intellectual, something of a dreamer, Ashley is also "as proficient as any of the other young men in the usual County diversions, hunting, gambling, dancing and politics, and was the best rider of them all."[19] In short, within his own world Ashley is perfect.

In the feudal society of the Old South, Twelve Oaks is the significant economic emblem, the splendid patriarchal property passed on from one generation to the next. Inherited property makes economic aggressiveness unnecessary and Ashley can have economic power without a display of threatening economic energy. Concomitantly, Ashley can maintain himself as hero without any display of

19. Margaret Mitchell, *Gone with the Wind* (New York: Macmillan, 1936), pp. 25–26.

sexual energy; with Scarlett, he is not the pursuer but the pursued. As the future master of Twelve Oaks and the object of the heroine's love, a hero whose powers are intrinsic and never overtly expressed, Ashley is clearly an echo of Darcy. But unlike Darcy, Ashley cannot sustain his role as hero; he cannot carry his role into the postwar world. He can, to be sure, remain a hero during the war when it seems that personal courage and loyalty and honor are all that matter. But this hero returns from the war vanquished, his loss of hero status emblemized by the destruction of Twelve Oaks.

Rhett Butler, conversely, carries all the distinguishing marks of conventional villainy. He is dark, marked with power rather than aristocratic languor, charged with sexuality. This is how he first appears to Scarlett.

> He looked quite old, at least thirty-five. He was a tall man and powerfully built. Scarlett thought she had never seen a man with such wide shoulders, so heavy with muscles, almost too heavy for gentility. When her eye caught his, he smiled, showing animal-white teeth below a close-clipped black mustache. He was dark of face, swarthy as a pirate, and his eyes were as bold and black as any pirate's appraising a galleon to be scuttled or a maiden to be ravished. There was a cool recklessness in his face and a cynical humor in his mouth as he smiled at her, and Scarlett caught her breath. She felt that she should be insulted by such a look and was annoyed with herself because she did not feel insulted. She did not know who he could be, but there was undeniably a look of good blood in his dark face. It showed in the thin hawk nose over the full red lips, the high forehead and the wide-set eyes.[20]

Any Victorian romance heroine would recognize in Rhett Butler the villain she must battle and destroy. A contemporary romance heroine would tremble at his power, coolness, and sexuality, but would set about domesticating him in order to free the hero from the veneer of villainy. Scarlett, to her own undoing, follows neither set of codes.

20. Ibid., p. 96.

Rhett Butler is also the representative man of the new economic order. The war that vanquishes Ashley destroys the economic system that nurtured his hero status. As Rhett observes early in the novel, the war will turn on the material superiority of one economic system over the other, and the North has a powerful advantage, Rhett declares, with its iron foundries and woolen mills and cotton factories and tanneries, with the "'thousands of immigrants who'd be glad to fight for the Yankees for food and a few dollars.'"[21] Yankee capitalism wins the war and brings a new economic system to the South. In this economic structure, Ashley as hero succumbs, giving way to Rhett, the new hero with the requisite vitality and aggressiveness to succeed.

But Rhett Butler is not like the hero of Harlequin romances, his apparent sins dissolving with confession. Rhett Butler has some distinctly unwholesome attributes. He has been ostracized in Charleston for "compromising" a girl and refusing to marry her. Much more significantly, he is thoroughly tainted by the capitalist marketplace; he is a war profiteer and, after the war, a business associate of carpetbaggers and scalawags. Mitchell wants us to see him clearly, unromantically, as a shrewd and amoral man, contemptuous of the values of the aristocratic antebellum world in which he was raised. Mitchell's achievement with Rhett Butler is that she elevates him to the status of hero without diminishing those other characteristics.

Rhett Butler's positive, heroic, qualities are his personal honesty, his absolute refusal of hypocrisy, his clear-sightedness, and his freedom from the anachronistic, debilitating conventions of Southern society. Moreover, he evidences a certain fineness in his own character through his recognition and respect for others of real quality of character—from Melanie to Mammy. But Rhett assumes the role of hero for other reasons as well, for his ability to wrest economic success out of the cataclysm of war and the debacle of Reconstruction. He is the first important hero of romance fiction to be allowed, and valued for, economic aggressiveness.

From the outset of *Gone with the Wind*, of course, Rhett expresses sexual energy, and by the middle of the novel that sexual power has

21. Ibid., pp. 110–11.

148

become united with economic power. The combination of sexual and economic power along with the dark, piratical handsomeness that marks Rhett Butler make him the direct descendant of the Victorian villain. But Margaret Mitchell, unlike Lewis and Fleming, directly acknowledges the fierce economic competition of the marketplace as the source of modern wealth. Discarding the fantasy of inheritance and ancestral homes, she discards as well their vitiated hero. Ashley is deposed, and the dark hero, his qualities of sexual and economic energy taken directly from the Victorian villain, is created for modern romance fiction.

Certainly, *Gone with the Wind* is not a romance, at least not as romance has been considered here. Mitchell is concerned to re-create an historical period, to paint a large social canvas. But in the triangle of the love story, romance elements are very powerful and significant. It is precisely because of the union of romance elements with the thick re-creation of an historical period that the transfer of roles between hero and villain becomes possible. Ashley, the perfect hero of romance, cannot survive in the real world of the postwar South. Weak and ineffective when he returns to Tara, he is entirely emasculated in Atlanta, where he works at Scarlett's mill, surviving on her forbearance.

As the heroine of the historical novel and the heroine of the romantic love story, Scarlett O'Hara is caught between altogether opposing value systems. Like the Victorian heroine, she sets out to control her own destiny in the aftermath of war. Back at Tara she undertakes man's responsibilities and man's work, for there are no men to assume these tasks. But for Scarlett no Victorian rescue is possible, there is no old gentleman to adopt and enrich her. Therefore, Scarlett passes beyond what is allowed the Victorian heroine; marrying for money, assuming the reins of business herself, and accepting the cutthroat measures necessary for success in this new economic order, she prospers.

But Scarlett remains trapped between romantic failure and economic success. Infatuated with Ashley and enamored of money, she fails to recognize the true hero of the story, a failure made especially ironic since the real hero's power derives from his ability, like hers, to survive in the postwar world. What is at stake here is too

149

important for Mitchell to allow her story resolution in the terms of a conventional happy ending. It takes Melanie's melodramatic death to bring Scarlett to a recognition of the truth: that Ashley had always loved Melanie, and that she, Scarlett, had simply created out of "the young horseman with his blond hair shining like a silver helmet,"[22] a fantasy hero. Scarlett is at last prepared to abandon that fantasy hero for the real one, the new hero of a new social order, but it is too late. Scarlett finds that Rhett no longer loves her, but more chilling is the discovery we make, that heroes, real heroes, are not immutable. In the final scene Rhett has altered, his body growing thick, his face coarsened, "no longer the head of a young pagan prince on new-minted gold but a decadent, tired Caesar on copper debased by long usage."[23]

As a heroine of romance, Scarlett fails. She loses the hero, punished for her economic aggressiveness, her fiercely heroic but finally unwomanly determination never to go hungry again, and for her consequent failure to discover the true hero. In romance, the first sin begets the second. This is a lesson the heroine of contemporary romance has taken very much to heart. Ashley has vanished from the story—his absence not even noted—and the heroine now devotes herself entirely to Rhett, finding in his arrogance and sexuality her true hero, and in the fruits of his economic aggressiveness all the money and power she will ever desire.

22. Ibid., p. 1016.
23. Ibid., pp. 1024–25.

6

ROMANCE AND SEXUAL POLITICS

Dear Ann Landers:

I am 20 years old, not beautiful, but no dog either. I have a peppy personality and am fun to be with.

Three weeks ago I came to work at this place as a waitress. My boss's son (I'll call him Rick) took an interest in me the third day of the job. He asked if he could take me home after work. I said yes. There was electricity between us the minute we met. He kissed me good night at the door and it was so wonderful I damn near fainted.

The next night Rick asked again if he could take me home. This time he wanted to stay and visit a little while. We ended up sleeping together.

For one solid week he never came near the restaurant. When he finally showed up he acted as if I were a stranger. I'm sure Rick likes me because we had such a great time together. I can't figure this whole thing out. Any ideas, Ann?

"Ann Landers," *Washington Post*, 23 August 1984

The bewildered young woman seeking help from Ann Landers tells the story of contemporary romance in its essential form. She is not beautiful, but spirited—"peppy." She has just begun a new job and met a man who is apparently her economic superior—the boss's son. There is "electricity" between them and their first kiss is so powerful she comes close to fainting. The "hero" pursues his sexual advantage, but there the young woman's story runs off the rails of romance formula. She accedes and he is lost to her. Although conventional wisdom and thousands of romance novels have warned her that the price of romantic love is paid in the coin of preserved virginity, she is baffled by the outcome of her adventure: "I can't figure this whole thing out." Ann Landers, of course, has no difficulty: "It sounds as if the sample was ample."

When the story of contemporary romance appears in such naked form, we seem to have returned to the world of *Pamela*, where nothing is demanded of the heroine but the preservation of her chastity and where unremitting vigilance in that task is rewarded with love and marriage to a man of wealth and status. In fact, today's popular romances ask a good deal more of the heroine and, in return, reward her more richly.

As fantasy literature, contemporary romance provides two kinds of gratification. In the story of sexual awakening, sexual conflict, and the resolution in love, it tells the fairy-tale story of a heroine's progress toward the rewards conventionally promised women—romantic love and marriage. At this level, the story is especially gratifying because the hero, the lover-husband, is himself a reflection of conventional fantasies; he is handsome, alluring, tender, and rich. In the subtext of romance a second fantasy is played out, a fantasy that subverts existing gender relations in the heroine's achieved mastery over the patriarchy, expressed in the fusion of economic power and sexuality, or—most often—in a merging of the two.

In the Victorian romances of May Agnes Fleming and Harriet Lewis important strategies are developed for allowing the heroine to triumph in both the surface story and the subtext. The essential strategy for their stories is the splitting of the male figure into three parts: the father-surrogate from whom the heroine could inherit the patrimony, the villain through whose destruction the heroine could extirpate male economic and sexual aggression, and the hero, who, purged of aggression, serves as the bland figure the heroine can join as wife in the conventional concluding marriage or reunion. The fantasy gratification afforded by these romances celebrates power at the expense of romantic love, a gratification that no longer suffices for contemporary romance.

For the Harlequin heroine the stakes, and the rewards, are different. It remains essential that she gain access to male power, but she is no longer willing to marry the vitiated shadow who satisfied the needs of her Victorian grandmother. The hero must now be invested with both sexual and economic power. Even when the heroine of contemporary romance, in some of the most recent variants of the story, is a successful businesswoman who has already inherited the patrimony in the form of her father's business, the hero must continue to be economically aggressive, successful, and powerful. The union of sexual and economic energy has not changed. What has altered is the weighting of the confused metaphorical relationship between them. For the Victorian villain, in whom these two aspects of his character go hand in hand, sexuality serves as a metaphor for the economic threat he poses. His desire to possess the heroine, however it first appears in the story, always becomes the desire to possess the inheritance. But in contemporary romance, it is the hero's economic power that supplies additional energy to his sexual power, as if his houses and cars, won in the competition of the marketplace, are metaphors for or manifestations of his sexual allure.

The most direct route to power, then, for the contemporary heroine is through the hero, the essence of whose power is expressed in sexuality. We have seen earlier that the Harlequin heroine, once awakened to sexuality, assumes the status of sexual being and, consequently, the sexual conflict becomes internalized; she battles her own attraction to the hero. In some very recent stories, the heroine goes beyond this, welcoming her sexuality and even finding it a means for bonding with the hero. Sexuality, of course, continues to be the arena for much of the conflict, even when it is not the sexual experience in itself that is threatening but instead the potential danger sexuality poses for the heroine in maintaining her competitive posture in some career or corporate situation.

As the heroine becomes a sexual being she can be seen as assuming to herself the significant element of male power. Still, a good deal of uncertainty and confusion remains, for female sexuality continues to be the evidence that leads her to a knowledge of her love for the hero, while male sexuality remains a force independent of love, at least until the heroine brings about a fusion of the two for the hero. That resolution, of course, satisfies several needs: the happy ending, the domestication of sexuality and concomitantly of male power, the triumph of the female principle of love. But at the same time, the deep contradiction inherent in this view of sexuality suggests that, for all the emphasis on eroticism in contemporary romance, female sexuality remains a very problematic area.

In its insistence on sexuality, contemporary romance finds a complicated and even confused response to real social conditions. The reemergence of the sexual woman in the twentieth century[1] and especially the effects of the sexual revolution of the 1960s have provided new models for female sexual behavior, but these models do not fit at all comfortably with long-established courtship practices. The "liberated woman" is, in fact, a highly suspect model for those

---

1. Mary Ryan argues that the reemergence of the woman as a sexual being at the end of the nineteenth century occurred because the "cherished nineteenth-century ideal of feminine purity had . . . outlived its usefulness" as a means of controlling "the economic lust and antisocial tendencies of the middle-class male." She does not, however, see a simple line of sexual development through this century, but instead a thirty-year period, from the 1890s to the 1920s, culminating in the "popular enthronement of sexuality," followed by a period of much reduced sexual expression during the Great Depression. After World War II, according to Ryan, Freudian and post-Freudian theory, especially in the work of Marie Robinson, Marie Bonaparte, and Helene Deutsch, refigured women's sexuality as passive, narcissistic, and masochistic, and as deriving its chief satisfaction in reproduction. The result was that in the 1950s women were directed "right back to where they had been a century earlier—in the captivity of the cult of motherhood" (*Womanhood in America: From Colonial Times to the Present*, 3d ed. [New York: Franklin Watts, 1983], pp. 221, 232–41, 251, 265–66).

who continue to look to marriage for economic security, for the crucial aspect of the popularized idea of the "liberated woman" is that the degree of her sexual self-determination is tied directly to the degree of her economic independence. The union of sexual and economic self-expression now becomes a characteristic of a particularly privileged female. But the obverse is equally true. For women who are not in a position to achieve economic independence, which is to say most women, sexual freedom is a chancy undertaking. Conventional wisdom continues to say—if perhaps only in a whisper—that chastity preserved promises the economic reward of marriage.

Still, in a society where sexuality is advertised overtly and covertly in every mass medium, it is impossible for a popular literary genre, whatever conservative morality it may espouse, to exist in a sexual vacuum and equally impossible for romance literature to replicate the moral strategies of Richardson's *Pamela*. For romance, the problem comes down to the fact that the principal effect of the sexual revolution on traditional courtship mores has been to stigmatize virginity as evidence of a woman's dedicated pursuit of matrimony. The new ideology of sexual freedom vulgarizes virginity as a transparent economic ploy with the result that an insistence on sexual purity has become an impossible stance for the romance heroine.

Despite the very recent romance stories that feature career women and even those with more explicit eroticism, the woman's movement is a problem, at least puzzling and very often threatening. Put most simply, the woman's movement threatens to leave women without their conventional support and mainstay in patriarchal society, that is, without the man who will provide economic maintenance. Although romance heroines have, for the last century, demonstrated their ability to survive independently and even to gain the patrimony independently, that success, a fantasy victory over male power, belongs to the subtext of romance. Real-world conditions, as the surface story makes clear, provide only one route to economic security: marriage is the heroine's only real recourse. From that vantage point, female sexuality is most threatening, for female sexuality as it develops in the heroine paradoxically threatens to defeminize her, just as economic aggressiveness itself challenges her ability to be-

156

come a real woman. In other words, to develop as a sexual being is to stand in jeopardy of losing the conventional qualities of femininity that are understood as the absolutely requisite attractions by which a woman can find a husband and assure herself of economic support. In an older, *Pamela*-like configuration, this situation would be reduced very simply to the fear of losing one's virginity and thus one's advantage in the marriage market. The stakes may be the same, but the underlying logic has shifted. And that logic stands in confused antithesis to a theme we have already seen as very powerfully at work in contemporary romance, the theme that presents the heroine's development into a sexual being as a means for assuming to herself some elements of male power.

Sexuality, as a result, is an intensely charged subject area for romance, the erotic component of these stories reflecting an obsessive need to cope with material that presents profound contradictions for women. It might be argued, of course, that the eroticism of contemporary romance is no more than a marketing device, but such an argument turns on itself. Popular romance is certainly sensitive to its market and its extraordinary success is a result of its ability to provide what that audience wants.[2] The charged and confused sexual material of romance reflects a cultural condition in which female sexuality has become a matter of profound significance and equally profound contradiction.

Romance fiction reflects this contradiction in the conflicting meanings and values it assigns to sexuality. On the one hand, contem-

2. The degree of explicit eroticism in any romance story depends on the series in which the story is published. Fairly recently Harlequin introduced one series called "Harlequin American Romance" and another called "Harlequin Temptation." Both series promise that they "explore today's new love relationships," and Harlequin Temptation novels add that "nothing is left unexplored. . . . You'll thrill to a candid new frankness as men and women seek to form lasting relationships in the face of temptations that threaten true love" (these quotes come from advertising material bound into 1984 Harlequin novels). "Silhouette Desire" is another series that offers more explicit sexuality. These stories "feature all of the elements you like to see in a romance, plus a more sensual, provocative story." "Silhouette Special Editions," published in a slightly longer format, "concentrate on romance in a longer, more realistic and sophisticated way, and they feature greater sensual detail" (these quotes are taken from the frontispiece material over the name of Karen Solem, Editor-in-Chief, in 1984 Silhouette novels).

porary romance makes sexuality an aspect of male power newly appropriated by the heroine. But at the same time romance fiction reflects a very anxious ambivalence about sexuality, not merely because the sexual drive of the hero signifies male power, but more crucially because the sexual response of the heroine threatens her essential femininity.

The ambivalence toward sexuality is especially apparent when the surface story of romance is seen as a story of initiation, for female sexuality establishes the terms under which the heroine's growth and maturation occur. As a ritual of female initiation, contemporary romance brings the heroine from girlhood to womanhood, conditions signified by the opposing states of single and married. In its aspect as initiation, contemporary romance presents its most conservative face, adhering rigorously to conventional attitudes about sexuality and about gender roles in general. Unlike Jane Eyre and unlike the heroines of Victorian romance, the heroines of today's romances do not manage to achieve some economic independence, some degree of power, that brings them to a state of symbolic equality with the hero. Even in those recent romances that present the heroine as a career woman, the achievement is understood as having occurred altogether independently of her growth to womanhood. Initiation takes place entirely along sexual-emotional lines. Initiation perforce occurs through the mentorship of the hero.

The hero's role in the heroine's initiation into womanhood reinforces sexual and emotional development as the crucial area in female initiation. The hero introduces the heroine to sexuality and serves as her erotic mentor through the story. The heroine, of course, has her own female area of power and knowledge; she is the representative of love, and the resolution of romance, as we have seen, finally domesticates passion as an aspect of love. But this cannot occur until the heroine, having completed her initiation, and under the conditions established by love, enters the state of womanhood. In other words, female sexuality becomes a necessary precondition for both womanhood and love. Considering that sexuality is a highly invested subject in romance, it is not surprising that the conception of the state of womanhood in these stories is, first of all, a state in which female sexuality is accepted and valued.

Sexuality may be the primary characteristic of womanhood in contemporary romance, but it is not the sole characteristic. The conservative aspect of romance fiction dominates the initiation theme and finds expression not only in the domestication of sexuality but in the secondary aspects of womanhood it presents as valuable. These aspects are thoroughly conventional, essentially qualities of tenderness, compassion, and selflessness. As she undergoes initiation, the romance heroine develops these qualities and, more significantly, abandons other characteristics inappropriate to womanhood. At the outset of the story, the heroine is a girl, and in that condition her behavior is marked by characteristics of willfulness, capriciousness, and hostility. The key term for such behavior in romance stories is "childish"; the heroine's initiation teaches her that she must relinquish her childishness.[3]

Considerable psychic energy is invested in the theme of heroine-as-child, a theme that serves several ends. As a child the heroine is innocent, both sexually and economically. That double innocence defends her against the charges leveled at the Other Woman, seen as sexually cynical and economically self-interested. The willful and capricious behavior of the childish heroine is much less odious, for in the first place, since such behavior is merely childish, it can be outgrown, and secondly, willful and capricious acts are intrinsically antithetical to the cold calculation necessary for cynical self-interest. Beyond that, as a child the heroine can receive her education at the hands of the hero, can be shaped into the perfect object of his desire. In this aspect, romance reenacts the Pygmalion myth, now told from the point of view of Galatea.

In conventional romances, the theme of the heroine-as-child can be useful in providing an ex post facto explanation for the hero's ambiguous behavior. In Patti Beckman's *Angry Lover*, the hero

3. Janice Radway has noted the childlike characteristics of the romance heroine, pointing out that the heroines in the romances her readers prefer serve "as symbolic representations of the immature female psyche. Although the women are unusually defiant in that they are capable of successfully opposing men, they are also characterized by childlike innocence and inexperience. . . . Moreover, these heroines are completely unaware that they are capable of passionate sexual urges" (*Reading the Romance: Women, Patriarchy and Popular Culture* [Chapel Hill: University of North Carolina Press, 1984], p. 126).

Vaulkhurst explains at the close of the story that "'I goaded and taunted you because I wanted you to learn to stand up for yourself, to discover who you are and become an independent adult.'"[4] In recent romance stories that present the heroine as a successful career woman, the theme takes on enhanced importance because of the necessity of demonstrating that success in the marketplace is in no way equivalent with maturity, that such success occurs independently of the initiation ritual popular romance reenacts. Romance stories of this type make it clear that independently successful women are emotionally jeopardized in their lack of sexual development. But the sexual and emotional stunting of such heroines is realized in these stories as a generalized childishness, always emotional and sometimes even intellectual.

A striking example is found in Jessica Ayre's *New Discovery*, whose heroine, mischievously named Clarissa Harlowe, is a published and prize-winning novelist. On first meeting her American publisher, the hero Garrett Hamilton, she loses her composure, marching out of his office and slamming the door behind her. Clarissa "cursed the man. He had made her behave like an unreasonable child." Soon, however, Clarissa stops blaming her childishness on Garrett. Although her outbursts and sulking come in response to his actions, the language of the story insists that this behavior is Clarissa's responsibility. This motif recurs throughout the story: "She sat rigidly in the corner of her seat, wondering how she could just have behaved with a childish surliness so inappropriate as to be embarrassing"; "She knew she sounded like a spoiled child, but she couldn't help herself"; "As if I were some temperamental child who needed to be cajoled! she thought to herself, admitting wryly that in part that was how she had behaved." And at the close of the book, returning to Garrett in New York, Clarissa recognizes that it will be difficult "to prove to him that despite her actions, she was reliable, not a silly, capricious child."[5]

4. Patti Beckman, *Angry Lover* (New York: Simon and Schuster, Silhouette Books, 1981), pp. 186–87.

5. Jessica Ayre, *New Discovery* (Toronto: Harlequin Books, 1984), pp. 10, 83, 89, 101, 174.

Garrett, of course, recognizes the childish elements in Clarissa and assumes the task of educating her, bringing her to maturity. The sexual nature of that education takes a special turn here, for Garrett believes that Clarissa's books lack the unique tension that sexual awareness brings. Their first sexual encounter comes in an editorial session when he kisses her to demonstrate the kind of vitality her hero lacks. In a later scene, when Clarissa tries to argue that her books are not about her life, Garrett responds enigmatically: "'No, not yet, that's true. They're still only about the child in you.'"[6]

One element in Clarissa's childishness is her attachment to her brother, to whom she writes long letters, "on [whose] pages . . . she lived her most intense life, her real life." When she accidentally meets him at the Frankfurt Book Fair, she is ecstatic. Half in jest she tells him there are no men in her life, for he has spoiled her for other men. The jest takes on a new edge when Garrett arrives and assumes her brother is a rival. But Clarissa has begun the passage from childhood to womanhood; when she joins her brother for dinner she finds that "for the first time in her life she couldn't quite bring herself to tell him about a part of herself." She keeps her feelings for Garrett a secret, "wanting to confide in [her brother], but somehow not being able to." For Clarissa, the "intrusion of a new reality" in their relationship "added a dimension of potential loneliness," but her brother is more realistic, noting "her mournful air" and telling her that she has to grow up sometime.[7]

Although Clarissa's maturation comes at Garrett's hands, the shock of growing up is reserved for her relationship with her brother. Having run away from Garrett and returned to England, she learns that her brother has a girlfriend: "A twinge of fear gripped her stomach at the thought of her encroaching isolation." But now Clarissa recognizes that this emotion belongs to childhood and she is "ashamed at her own childishness."[8] Maturity, in this story, is clearly tied to separation from the world of childhood affections and there is a strong suggestion that mature love differs from child-

6. Ibid., p. 114.
7. Ibid., pp. 22, 104.
8. Ibid., p. 164.

like love specifically in its sexual component. The heroine must surrender one to win the other.[9]

The romance heroine relinquishes childish behavior in favor of womanly behavior, specifically tenderness and compassion and the ability to assume the role of nurturer. Typically, romance stories signal the heroine's maturation into the role of nurturing woman as a moment when she sees the hero through new eyes, perceiving him suddenly as tired, drawn, overworked. This change in the heroine's perception of the hero demonstrates her new capacity for caring, very often by specifically pointing to her acknowledgment and appreciation of his responsibilities in the male arena of work. In *New Discovery*, aware for the first time that Garrett looks tired, "gaunt," Clarissa's perception of him changes: "[It] suddenly occurred to Clarissa that despite the calm with which he usually met her, the time he gave her, he drove himself hard. . . . The thought made her feel that she had been excessively selfish, so immersed in her own work, her own emotions, that she had somehow assumed that Garrett, as an editor . . . existed only for her."[10]

Only rarely does the romance heroine actually provide nurturing for the hero; the perception of his need and vulnerability is adequate evidence for her surrender of childish egotism in favor of womanly selflessness. Before this happens, as if to emphasize the charm of childhood and, consequently, the magnitude of the heroine's sacrifice, romance fiction allows her the experience of *being* nurtured. In a very dramatic shift of gender roles, it is the hero who acts as nurturer, most often through scenes of feeding and secondarily

9. Not all emotional links to childhood are as benign as Clarissa's affection for her brother. Often the heroine is emotionally scarred, harboring feelings of bitterness and hostility that must be outgrown, again under the tutelage of the hero. When the hero of Ariel Berk's *Promise of Love* proposes to the heroine, he does so on the condition that she resume relations with her parents. They had cut her off emotionally when she married against their will; now widowed three years, the heroine continues to nurse her rage at them. But the hero will not tolerate such childish behavior; he wants his parents and hers to witness their wedding. " 'Parents are important, Carla, and you've been without yours for too long. Pride isn't much of a substitute for parents. I want you to make up with them. I want you to invite them to our wedding' " ([New York: Simon and Schuster, Sillhouette Books, 1984], p. 186).

10. Ayre, *New Discovery*, p. 94.

in providing comfort—bath and bed—to the heroine rescued from some physical peril. As well as dramatizing the cost of the heroine's surrender of childhood, the nurturing male provides a particularly powerful fantasy, tying the hero's love to actions conventionally associated only with woman's love.[11]

Even the most apparently fierce and brutal heroes are capable of nurture. The hero in *Angry Lover* rescues the heroine from a storm in the Big Bottom, and though he scolds her for her childishness in exposing herself to such danger, soon comforts her with food: "Delicious aromas wafted from the silver tray Clement was holding. He brought it into her room and arranged it on a table. When he uncovered the dishes, she saw a golden omelette, crisp bacon, piles of toast, jelly, a bowl of fresh fruit, and a pot of rich, steaming coffee." Moreover, when the heroine needs nurture, the hero is careful not to offer sex. In *Angry Lover*, the tray of food is followed by a scene of sexual talk, but only talk, for the heroine needs to rest from her adventure. The hero kisses her "tenderly" and says, " 'You have a rest now. Have a good night's sleep.' "[12]

The nurturing hero is a fairly new element in romance, finding its source in Margaret Mitchell's Rhett Butler, the economically powerful and sensual hero whose masculinity would seem to preclude the possibility of nurturing behavior. But when he and Scarlett marry, we discover his great capacity for compassionate caring. The marriage of Scarlett and Rhett is presented in terms that are to become familiar as those associated in contemporary romance with early-marriage stories. Although this is Scarlett's third mar-

11. In *Reading the Romance*, Janice Radway finds in nurturing a theme central to the powerful fantasy gratification afforded by romance fiction. Adopting Nancy Chodorow's conception of the development of female personality, Radway argues for the ability of romance to provide for readers the experience of nurturance they, as society's nurturers, no longer enjoy. For these romance readers "the fantasy . . . evokes the memory of a period in the reader's life when she was the center of a profoundly nurturant individual's attention." Romance, thus, grants "a utopian vision in which female individuality and a sense of self are shown to be compatible with nurturance and care by another." The power of this vision lies in the displacement of nurturing from the woman as mother to the man as lover, offering the reader "a temporary but literal denial of the demands women recognize as an integral part of their roles as nurturing wives and mothers" (pp. 84 and 97).

12. Beckman, *Angry Lover*, pp. 150–51.

riage and although she and Rhett have a child together, real marriage, as romance understands it, is never achieved: the heroine fails to acknowledge her love for the hero and he will not confess his love for her.

Having failed to understand her passionate response to Rhett's lovemaking as the sign of her love for him, Scarlett remains a child, and as a child, she is the recipient of Rhett's nurturing. "Some mornings [Rhett] dismissed the maid and brought her the breakfast tray himself and fed her as though she were a child." When Scarlett experiences the recurring nightmare of her return to Tara, a nightmare of desolation, starvation, and terror, Rhett provides nurturing comfort. "Rhett was leaning over her when she woke, and without a word he picked her up in his arms like a child and held her close, his hard muscles comforting, his wordless murmuring soothing, until her sobbing ceased." Absolved of all adult responsibility, for herself as well as for others, the nurtured heroine enters a world of absolute security. As Rhett explains to Scarlett, " 'if you get used to being safe and warm and well fed in your everyday life, you'll stop dreaming that dream. And, Scarlett, I'm going to see that you are safe.' " [13]

Romance fiction maintains a discreet silence about the future nurturing of the heroine. As the heroine passes from childhood to womanhood, it becomes appropriate to the conservative theme of initiation that she assume the nurturing role, and her perception of the hero as tired, overworked, in need of nurture himself, signals her readiness for that role. But specific acts of nurturing are not required of the heroine, and in their absence, the fantasy of the nurturing hero, with its powerful reversal of gender roles, remains at least a possibility.

By enhancing the character of the hero, the theme of male nurturing serves a further function in contemporary romance: it makes the heroine's success in winning such a man all the more wonderful. This hero, handsome, sensual, and rich, is the harbor of perfect safety, economic and emotional; he satisfies all needs, provides af-

13. Margaret Mitchell, *Gone with the Wind* (New York: Macmillan, 1936), pp. 854, 856.

fection, passion, money, power, tenderness. Such a prize must be deserved. The heroine must somehow earn it.

In Richardson's *Pamela*, the preservation of the heroine's virginity is sufficient means for gaining the hero. But since Pamela's time, the hero has become a figure invested with extraordinary glamour and equally extraordinary value. His descent from Jane Austen's Darcy and Charlotte Brontë's Rochester through the villain of Victorian romance and his redemption as hero in Margaret Mitchell's Rhett Butler has taken the contemporary romance hero a long way from Richardson's Lord B. As a result, earning this hero is a good deal more complicated a task than Pamela faced.

Contemporary romance not only establishes the hero, in his sexual and economic power, as someone worth earning, it also refuses to compromise that victory. Unlike Elizabeth Bennet, today's romance heroine never loses her economic innocence; she will not acknowledge the erotic appeal of the hero's economic power. And unlike Jane Eyre, she will not accept a hero whose economic power is in any way diminished; his physical property comes to her intact. And unlike the heroine of Victorian romance, she will not settle for economic power alone, eradicating sexual power in the destruction of the villain and settling into marriage with a tame and sexless hero. Although the contemporary heroine does eliminate the threat of the hero's sexuality through the power of love, her marriage to him promises a future rich in sexuality.

Given the sublimely satisfying hero of romance and the heroine's refusal to compromise her success, what does contemporary romance require of her in return for what she wins? What are the costs of the heroine's victory?

A good many feminist critics have shown us that the portrayal of women in literature is generally a reflection of sacrifice and powerlessness.[14] Romance fiction, as a form of popular literature, is no

14. Jean Kennard, in her study of the two-suitor convention in Victorian fiction, finds the convention itself an instrument of female betrayal. In *Victims of Convention* she points out that the heroine's marriage to the hero represents "the adjustment of the protagonist to society's values, a condition which is equated with maturity," and maturity, according to Kennard, comes with the acceptance of "male reality" and the concomitant surrender of the heroine's essential selfhood. "Since in order

exception; at the very least, the heroines of these stories are seen as having embraced passivity. For example, Kathryn Weibel, in *Mirror, Mirror: Images of Women Reflected in Popular Culture*, sees passivity as the essential characteristic of women in popular literature, and she relates the passivity of the heroine directly to her perceived separation from the world of work. The image of women in popular

to reach maturity the heroine must accept certain values and since the repository of those values is, according to convention, the right suitor, at the end of the novel she invariably appears to have subordinated her own personality to that of the hero. . . . The very structure of the novel places him as leader, her as follower. For her, maturity lies in learning that her ideas are fantasies, that happiness lies in approximating the male reality and in denying much of what had seemed to be herself" ([Hamden, Conn.: Archon Books, 1978], p. 14).

A number of other critics see Austen's Elizabeth Bennet and Brontë's Jane Eyre as among the heroines who have sold their independence, even their selfhood, as the price they pay for winning Darcy and Rochester. An extreme example can be found in *The Madwoman in the Attic*, where Sandra Gilbert and Susan Gubar talk of the painful lessons of subordination Elizabeth Bennet must learn before she can be united with Darcy. They argue that Austen dramatized "the necessity of female submission for female survival," thereby creating a story "flattering to male readers because it describes the taming not just of any woman but specifically of a rebellious, imaginative girl who is amorously mastered by a sensible man." Like other Austen heroines, specifically Emma and Marianne, Elizabeth undergoes "mortification," seen as "the necessary accompaniment to the surrender of self-responsibility and definition" (*The Madwoman in the Attic: the Woman Writer and the Nineteenth Century Imagination* [New Haven: Yale University Press, 1979], pp. 154, 163). But this is polemic, not analysis. To see in Elizabeth's period of trial and in her consequent reassessment of her values, her "prejudices" to use Austen's term, a "surrender of self-responsibility and definition," and to ignore altogether Darcy's own personal reassessment and his dramatic demonstration of his new value system in his rescue of Lydia, is to lose sight of the structure and the language of Austen's novel.

More balanced appraisals, however, also point to the cost necessarily borne by the heroine in her winning of the hero. In relation to *Jane Eyre*, Patricia Spacks addresses the maiming of Rochester as what "makes possible a marriage of ideal reciprocity," but adds that "Rochester, even crippled, remains the strong male on whom a woman can safely and happily depend, to whom she will willingly submit" (*The Female Imagination* [New York: Alfred A. Knopf, 1975], p. 66.)

Francoise Basch, pointing to the "independence, energy, the habit of relying on one's own resources" that mark Jane Eyre, sees these characteristics, along with her moral superiority, as what make it possible for her, like Brontë's other heroines, to combine "submission and respect toward the loved man." Submission remains an essential element in Brontë's "imaginary world, of impassioned women seeking a virile and ferocious master" (*Relative Creatures: Victorian Women in Society and the Novel* [New York: Schocken Books, 1974], pp. 163, 165, 169).

culture, she argues, is a "middle-class image reflective of the role assigned women under the division of labor created by the industrial revolution." The passivity of women in popular fiction, however, is not confined to her role in the world of work, extending beyond that to her role in romance novels: "Despite the fact that romance is virtually the only adventure that literature allows to females, the romance heroine has standardly been, as critic Joanna Russ puts it, a passive protagonist." [15]

Certainly, passivity cannot be attributed to the Victorian heroines in the fiction of Harriet Lewis and May Agnes Fleming; we have seen those heroines assuming masculine ambitions and undertaking masculine adventures on their way to money and power, usually in direct conflict with the villain. Through their aggressive heroines, these writers, like the English sensation novelists Elaine Showalter writes of, express "a wide range of suppressed female emotions . . . tapping and satisfying fantasies of protest and escape." [16] But the contemporary heroine presents a different problem.

The heroine of today's romance novels is not thrust into a conflict between good and evil as emblemized by the opposing male figures of hero and villain. Without that opposition, without the isolated evil male figure, this heroine has no one with whom to do battle, no one to best in an overt struggle for dominance. With the Victorian hero and villain conflated into the single figure of the contemporary romance hero, the heroine's action and goal change radically. Her task in today's romance fiction is one of discovery, learning to recognize the hero beneath whatever mask he may affect.

The heroine's task, then, is real, but it is not a task that demands outward energy of purpose. It is not precisely that the heroine has been reduced to passivity, but that her actions have become inter-

15. Kathryn Weibel, *Mirror, Mirror: Images of Women Reflected in Popular Culture* (Garden City, N.Y.: Anchor Books, 1977), pp. xi–xii. Janice Radway, too, argues for passivity as an element of romance, but for Radway it is not a question of the passive heroine but of passivity as the desired goal of the narrative itself, "the creation of that perfect union" with "the ideal male . . . masculine and strong, yet nurturant too" (*Reading the Romance*, p. 97).

16. Elaine Showalter, *A Literature of Their Own: British Women Novelists from Brontë to Lessing* (Princeton, N.J.: Princeton University Press, 1977), p. 159.

nalized. Because the problem of discovering the hero's true nature is not the stuff of adventure, the contemporary heroine is removed from the world of action to the world of psychology, her focus is entirely inward, her attention trained on her own emotions and on the puzzling and ambiguous character of the hero. As a result the contemporary romance heroine leads an active, even a frenetic, internal life, her problem less passivity than a kind of emotional claustrophobia.

More dramatic gestures of self-denial than passivity are also attributed to the romance heroine as the high price she pays for her success in winning the hero. Criticism of popular romance sees the subordination of selfhood as particularly significant because it is a price paid not only by the heroine of romance stories but by the reader, through her identification with the heroine.[17]

Contemporary romance is not unique in eliciting critical notice of the sexism implicit in the self-subordination of the heroine; however, the submissiveness of the heroine of contemporary romance is seen as going far beyond that attributed to the heroines of classic fiction like *Pride and Prejudice* and *Jane Eyre*. Criticism of popular romance understands the heroine as paying a much heavier cost, her submission extending to masochistic self-betrayal. These assessments are based on the heroine's emotional responses to the hero, on the ritually repetitive elements of the romance story line that emotionally imperil the heroine. The heroine is threatened on two sides. First, she is in danger of acceding to the hero's sexual allure, and, even more threateningly, to her own sexual response. And second, she is in danger of failing to understand that the hero's behavior, however puzzling, is the expression of love. Both elements of the formula take their toll on the heroine, who seems to ricochet between the hero's sexual behavior, which lures her closer to him, and the hero's other-than-sexual behavior, which drives her away from him. Such

17. Ann Douglas has called contemporary popular romances "dramas of dependency" ("Soft-Porn Culture," *The New Republic* [30 August 1980]: 25–29). Tania Modleski charges Harlequin romances with female "self-betrayal" (*Loving with a Vengeance: Mass-Produced Fantasies for Women* [Hamden, Conn.: Archon Books, 1982], p. 37).

an emotional roller coaster seems to reduce the heroine utterly to the condition of victim, and it is essentially that appearance of victimization that leads commentators to see the romance heroine as masochistically cooperating in the betrayal of her own selfhood, as embracing a pathological passivity so intense as to become what Tania Modleski shrewdly calls the "disappearing act." [18]

The significance of these elements of romance formula, however, should not be exaggerated. Without question, to the limited extent that romances invest psychic energy in the development of character, these events have the effect of powerfully demoralizing the heroine. But insofar as romance reenacts ritual, they must be understood as requisite stages in the heroine's initiation and, therefore, less as psychic traumas than as ritual experiences she must undergo on her way to womanhood and success. This in no way suggests that these emotional adventures are to be overlooked or exonerated, far less approved. The point is that they are reflexes within the text of underlying assumptions about women's roles in society and that it is those premises that require examination.

Three interconnected assumptions about women stand at the heart of contemporary romance: first, the fact of woman's socioeconomic inferiority in the marketplace, her powerlessness; second, as a corollary of the first, the severe limits placed on women's means for self-development both socioeconomically and personally, limits that restrict personal development almost entirely to emotional development, to emotional self-expression; and third, given the consequent overvaluation of the expression of the emotional self, woman's potential for emotional victimization, her psychological vulnerability. No feminist could quarrel with this assessment of woman's status in our society. The problem lies in the fact that popular romance fiction accepts this assessment as a given, as unchanged and unchanging. Rather than attempting to remake society, romance fiction offers the fantasy of woman's economic victory within the contraints of that society as well as the added gratification that comes

18. Modleski; "The Disappearing Act: Harlequin Romances," title for chapter 2, *Loving with a Vengeance*.

with making that victory an act of vengeance in the domesticating of the hero insofar as he stands for male power in a patriarchal society.[19]

Seen from this point of view, the foregrounding of sexuality in romance fiction assumes a new complexity. It is, for one thing, worth noting that romance shares with radical feminist theory an insistence on the centrality of female sexuality. Certainly, romance comes to different conclusions, finds resolution in turning female sexuality into an instrument of love and monogamous marriage. What is significant, however, is not the conservative uses romance makes of female sexuality, but the fact that romance has had to come to terms with it in the first place.

The sexual content of romance fiction, as has been noted earlier, is widely seen as offering an erotic lure to readers, as providing a kind of female pornography with masochistic overtones. But whatever erotic pleasures romance may or may not offer, the sexual material is surely not limited to that purpose. Scenes of sexual temptation and arousal may occur and recur in romance, apparently establishing the content of these fictions as scenes of sexual arousal and consummation do in pornography. Nevertheless, the reading of romance reveals very different tensions and resolutions. As Jeffrey Weeks points out, "the fact that . . . various cultures share general sexual forms . . . does not mean that their content, inner structures and meanings are identical."[20] The same point can well be made in regard to various forms within the same culture, especially in regard to mass-market fictions like pornography and romance, produced for altogether different audiences.

In his book, *Sex, Politics and Society*, Weeks joins Foucault and others in challenging an essentialist view of sexuality. Adopting Foucault's assertion that the idea of sexuality "is an historical construct of the past few hundred years," Weeks then challenges Fou-

19. Janice Radway makes the same observation about the romance readers she studies in *Reading the Romance*: "The Smithton women are, in sum, significantly more inclined than their feminist critics to recognize the inevitability and reality of male power and the force of social convention to circumscribe a woman's ability to act in her own interests" (p. 78.)

20. Jeffrey Weeks, *Sex, Politics and Society: The Regulation of Sexuality since 1800* (New York: Longman's, 1981), p. 11.

cault's privileging of the notion of "discourse" as itself ahistorical. Discourses, he argues, are not "the only contact with the real; they have their conditions of existence and their effects in concrete historical, social, economic and ideological situations." Popular romance is itself a discourse on sexuality, specifically female sexuality, and as such it has its sources in the concrete historical situation of women in bourgeois society. Like more radical feminist discourse, romance finds its subject at the heart of the contradictions facing women in that society. Unlike radical feminism, it settles for unradical solutions.[21]

The solutions romance arrives at in the surface story of love, and in what I have called the sexual plot, are profoundly conservative. Such solutions can be seen, in fact, as the presentation in the form of fiction of George Gilder's view of gender relations. In *Sexual Suicide*, Gilder's attack on feminist theory and practice takes the form of smooth flattery for "natural" womanhood and adopts a tone of awed humility before the power of that womanhood. Men may control "the economy of the marketplace," but this is a meager triumph compared to women, who control "the economy of eros." The ironies of that astonishing phrase elude Gilder. Straight-faced, he claims for women a special kind of polymorphous sexuality, encompassing pregnancy, "the tumult of childbirth," and nursing. Men are poor "sexual outsiders and inferiors," for whom sex is "an indispensable test of identity." Since this is not true for women, since for women there is a special and necessary "connection between orgasm and extended emotional ties," promiscuous sex for women "ordinarily represents a more significant violation of love."[22]

Gilder's woman and the heroine of romance are the same; the very principle of "love" resides in both. Moreover, both understand their obligation to human culture: "the crucial process of civilization is the subordination of male sexual impulses and psychology to long-term horizons of female biology."[23] In this immense project the domestication of the hero of romance takes on historical resonance.

21. Ibid., pp. 6 and 11.
22. George Gilder, *Sexual Suicide* (New York: Quadrangle, 1973), pp. 14–25.
23. Ibid., p. 23.

The preservation of the family becomes demystified in Barbara Ehrenreich's discussion of antifeminist backlash to the feminist movement and especially to ERA. In *The Hearts of Men* she strips love from the discussion to lay bare its economic face. It is not "the economy of eros" that is in question, but the economics of gender. Ehrenreich sees the female opponents of ERA as profoundly frightened by a sexual revolution that would "dislodge a husband from his marriage and catapult his ex-wife into sudden, midlife downward mobility." In the face of this threat, love is altogether inadequate; only law will suffice. Ehrenreich cites Phyllis Schlafly, who warns women that love will not serve to keep their husbands loyal to the task of supporting them; law alone will maintain the economics of traditional marriage. The view of gender relations that is drawn by conservatives is one of "a permanent state of war," concludes Ehrenreich: "The interests of the sexes are irreconcilably opposed; the survival of women demands the subjugation of men."[24]

In romance, survival and subjugation are metamorphosed back into love; the economics of marriage are masked, as are the anxieties of women, and dissolved in the fantasy resolution of each story. Insofar as romance echoes the dominant ideology, it places sexuality squarely in the service of love, love in the service of marriage, and marriage in the service of status quo economic relations between the genders.

But this does not altogether exhaust the treatment of female sexuality in romance fiction. Despite the conservative ends that sexuality is made to serve in romance and despite the contradictions it at once negotiates and reinforces, romance manages to make sex not only the heroine's major problem, the heart of her dilemma, the source of her suffering, but also a source of pleasure.

Jeffrey Weeks traces the changes in the images and roles assigned

24. Barbara Ehrenreich, *The Hearts of Men: American Dreams and the Flight from Commitment* (Garden City, N.Y.: Anchor Press, 1983), pp. 147 and 168. Mary Ryan comments that the New Right had "calculated that appeals to the family anxieties of American citizens reaped popular support and financial contributions." Their "campaign to defend the family would make good sense to the many women whose own welfare and comfort [were] still bound up with their marital status. From a pragmatic perspective, a 'pro-family' policy seemed in the best short-term interest of many women" (*Womanhood in America*, pp. 335–36).

women over the last thirty years and observes a process of sexual-
ization of women, "constructing a female sexuality to accord with a
series of major social developments." By the 1960s "a redefinition of
female sexuality" was taking place, specifically, "in terms of its possibilities for pleasure, for enjoyment unbounded by the old exigencies of compulsory childbirth or endless domestic chores."[25] It is that
new definition of sexual pleasure that romance fiction incorporates.

The fantasy pleasures of romance foreground female sexuality,
privilege female sexuality. This is true in the fictions themselves and
even in whatever erotic pleasures the audience may find in them. To
be sure, the dynamics of romance hedge these pleasures round with
cautions and conditions. The status quo is unchanged. But the point
remains that romance fiction presents a new image of women to a
huge public, a role model who can find pleasure as a sexual being,
and at the same time manage and channel sexuality—both female
and male—into the accepted path of love and marriage.

Romance fiction negotiates this tricky path as the essential strategy for redeeming women's powerlessness and vulnerability under
the economic conditions of the patriarchy and at the same time belies
those conditions in the masked subtext of economic vengeance and
appropriation. Moreover, romance fiction presents this victory as
one that incurs no real cost to the heroine, including even the emotional battering she has undergone. That experience lies entirely
behind her when the story reaches its resolution; moreover, it is
completely explained away, rationalized, given shape and meaning as a necessary part of the discovery of love. The resolution
of romance promises that once love is discovered and acknowl-
edged, emotional battering, having served its purpose, need never
occur again. More important, the disadvantages the heroine has
lived under, as an essentially disenfranchised member of patriarchal
society, are made to vanish. Married to the hero, sharing in his
sexuality and his wealth, she is no longer powerless. And having
brought the hero to a belief in love, her own emotional jeopardy is
neutralized, for her emotional life is now in the hands of a male who
has himself been redeemed by love.

25. Weeks, *Sex, Politics and Society*, p. 258.

Romance fiction, as it traces the ritually repetitive story of each heroine's accession to love and power, entirely rationalizes the emotional suffering of the heroine. Nevertheless, that emotional suffering is made the central aspect of each heroine's experience; the obsession with sexuality that marks romance is equally an obsession with the emotional toll that sexuality exacts. In part, this obsessive fascination is accounted for by the complex and confused role we have seen sexuality play in romance fiction. In part, it comes about as the result of the intensely protected economic innocence of the heroine of today's romances. In *Pride and Prejudice*, Jane Austen establishes conflict between interest and affect, resolving them in the person of Darcy who combines both attractions. But since Austen, writers have become increasingly modest about interest, about allowing their heroines to acknowledge the lure of property. In contemporary fiction, the hero's economic power is continually manifested but fiercely denied as a source of attraction. It is property rather than sexuality that has become unmentionable.

Reflecting the conditions established for courtship and marriage in bourgeois society, fiction has developed an intimate, but continually shifting, connection between sexual and economic power. In the earliest examples, these two expressions of power are distributed "fairly": the male holds economic power and the female, sexual power, specifically the power to withhold sexuality, to preserve her virginity, her principal commodity in the marriage market. This is the power relationship we find in *Pamela*. But very soon fiction begins to redistribute sexual power, displacing it from the female to the male. It is Rochester, not plain Jane Eyre, who is fascinating and alluring, and while the heroines of Victorian romances mature into beautiful women, it is the center of male energy, the villain, who radiates sexual power. Contemporary romances continue in this tradition, allowing for pretty and occasionally even beautiful heroines, but dwelling on the intense sexual attractiveness of the hero.

The displacement of sexual allure from the heroine to the hero and the concomitant muting of the heroine's beauty represent a denial of female beauty as a source of power for the heroine. That denial, in turn, suggests a profound uneasiness about beauty and its uses. In fact, as Lois Banner discovers in *American Beauty*, by

174

the early nineteenth century a belief in the power of female beauty "to attract wealthy and powerful men into marriage," the power, that is, to effect women's economic advancement, had created "a Cinderella mythology," which served as "the counterpart of the self-made-man mythology for men." During the century, beauty became increasingly disassociated from moral goodness, allowing for a new definition of beauty, "one more concerned with sensuality and with surface features of face and body as a way of attracting men." Such beauty, finally, "represented not morality, but *power*" [emphasis mine].[26]

The transfer of sexual allure and sexual power from the heroine to the hero accomplishes the surrender of the heroine's only source of power in bartering for marriage as upward mobility. It also makes possible a system of profound disguises and denials in romance fiction. By displacing sexual power from the heroine to the hero, romance fiction insists absolutely on the powerlessness, and hence the purity of the heroine. Purity, moreover, is not only sexual, but more significantly, economic, and it is this overdetermined innocence that provides the central emblem of the heroine's powerlessness and, therefore, her virtue. In part, her virtue defends her against the charge of calculation and self-interest. At the same time, it dissociates her from patriarchal society, where power is instinct with the evil of the system itself. In such a society, powerlessness alone can be virtuous; the less the power, the greater the virtue. Thus, the heroine, already doubly denied power, is made to seem yet more innocent and weak in comparison to, and at the mercy of, the dominance of the hero, the potency of his authority, his economic power, now enhanced by sexual power as well.

The emotional suffering the heroine of contemporary romance fiction undergoes serves as the final element in the complex defense against the charge of economic self-interest. Having relinquished sexual power to the hero, she becomes at last the victim of that power, for what beauty and allure do remain to the heroine are themselves turned against her. The innocent heroine's modest

26. Lois W. Banner, *American Beauty* (Chicago: University of Chicago Press, 1984), pp. 10–14.

beauty, romance argues, is no advantage, no snare to trap a husband, but instead a liability, imperiling her as it serves to arouse the hero's lust. In this way, the defense romance mounts to preserve the economic innocence of the heroine brings sexuality as an element in bourgeois courtship full circle. If women were once popularly believed to have two objects to bring to barter in the marriage market, their beauty—that is, their sexual allure—and their virginity, the displacement of sexual allure onto the hero of romance not only reduces woman's currency to the coin of virginity alone, but threatens that virginity itself with the very sexual allure she has surrendered to the hero.

Critical displeasure with contemporary romance has located its distasteful elements in the obsessive attention paid to sexuality, in the emotionally victimized heroine, and in the apparently brutal hero. But in the strategies of romance all three play crucial functions and all three are somehow rationalized, "accounted for," in the resolution of the story and in the fantasy gratification it provides. The deep flaw of romance fiction lies elsewhere, lies in the ultimate failure of romance to provide, even in fantasy, a satisfying answer to the problem of women's powerlessness.

Romance fiction insists so heavily on the powerlessness of its heroine precisely because it exists to redress, in fantasy, the powerlessness of women in bourgeois society. What romance provides by way of gratification, it first denies. Thus, despite the formulaic simplicity of any individual romance story, the genre itself is rife with the complexities and contradictions that arise from the simultaneous urge to mask women's desires and to gratify them, as well as from the related necessity to reinforce conventional values in the surface story of initiation and at the same time subvert the patriarchal order in the subtext of vengeance and appropriation.

Romance finally fails because the contradictions between the surface story and the subtext are too powerful to be resolved. The fantasy gratification provided by the surface story is tied to conventional values, bound up with conservative goals of love and marriage. But the fantasy gratification afforded by the subtext is altogether subversive of such values and goals. The story of initiation resolves in the achievement of conventional womanhood. The story

176

of vengeance and the appropriation of power resolves in the denial of the values of conventional womanhood, values adopted whole-sale from the patriarchy. Romance attempts to have it both ways; it seeks in marriage to the supremely attractive and powerful hero the answer to woman's powerlessness, but in doing so it decon-structs itself through an unanswerable contradiction: to reestablish the power relations between men and women through love and marriage is finally to accede to the conditions imposed by patri-archal society. Marriage remains woman's sole means of access to power, and romantic love—the supreme value in romance fiction—relentlessly defends women against economic self-interest in mar-riage. Thus, romance ends where it began, its resolution endlessly reenacting the contradiction it exists to dispel.

INDEX

Adams, Tracy: *The Moth and the Flame*, 29, 32, 61
Aries, Phillippe, 131n
Austen, Jane: *Pride and Prejudice*, 4, 11, 22, 133–41, 142, 143, 144, 147, 165, 166n, 174
Ayre, Jessica: *New Discovery*, 109n, 160–62

Banner, Lois, 174–75
Basch, Francoise, 166n
Baym, Nina, 72
Beckman, Patti: *Angry Lover*, 24, 26, 29, 32, 33, 51n, 159–60, 163
Berk, Ariel: *Promise of Love*, 116n, 121n, 162n
Bourgeois society, 128, 129–32, 135, 146–49. *See also* Social class
Brontë, Charlotte: *Jane Eyre*, 4, 11, 51–57, 59, 65, 70, 141–43, 144–45, 146, 165, 166n, 174
Brontë, Emily: *Wuthering Heights*, 51n
Browning, Dixie: *East of Today*, 109, 112

Calder, Jenni, 8n
Cawelti, John, 15
Chambers, Ginger: *Passion's Prey*, 122
Clair, Daphne: *Never Count Tomorrow*, 60–61, 105
Collins, Susanna: *Flamenco Nights*, 26, 29, 44n, 109n
Comic tradition, 19–20, 30–31
Cott, Nancy, 75n

Crane, Stephen: *Maggie, A Girl of the Streets*, 102

Defoe, Daniel: *Moll Flanders*, 37, 103
Degler, Carl, 75n, 98n, 104n
Douglas, Ann, 16n, 168n
Dreiser, Theodore: *Sister Carrie*, 102

Edwards, Paula: *Bewitching Grace*, 23–24, 33, 44n, 51n, 109
Ehrenreich, Barbara, 46–47, 172

Fantasy, 3, 5, 6, 7, 8, 12, 18, 36, 131, 132, 133, 141, 145, 153, 169–70, 173, 176–77
Father (also Surrogate father), 59–62, 69, 79, 81, 91–92, 117, 120–22, 123, 144–45; of hero, 59–62, 144–45. *See also* Incest motif; Patriarchy
Faust, Beatrice, 16n
Firth, Suzanna: *Dark Encounter*, 28, 31–32
Fleming, May Agnes, 4, 11, 71–72, 73–78, 80, 82, 83–84, 90–91, 95–99, 107, 108–9, 144–45, 146, 153–54, 165–67; *The Actress' Daughter*, 63, 84–89, 99, 107; *Carried by Storm*, 99–100, 101; *Guy Earlscourt's Wife*, 97; *The Heir of Charlton*, 97; *Norine's Revenge*, 81, 99; *Sybil Campbell*, 82–83; *Who Wins?*, 100–101
Foucault, Michel, 170–71
Frye, Northrop, 7, 18–19, 21, 26–27, 134n

Gilbert, Sandra, 166n
Gilder, George, 171–72
Gothic tradition, 56, 58, 135
Gubar, Susan, 166n

Hastings, Brooke: *Innocent Fire*, 44n,
  109
Heath, Stephen, 17n, 35

Incest motif, 60–61, 78–80

Jameson, Fredric, 7, 12

Kelley, Mary, 72, 73n, 76
Kelly, Joan, 50n, 73
Kennard, Jean, 56n, 136n, 165
Kessler-Harris, Alice, 98n, 104n
Kidd, Flora: *A Personal Affair*, 29, 32

Lamb, Charlotte: *Retribution*, 27–28,
  32, 52n, 109
Lewis, Harriet, 4, 11, 70–71, 73–78,
  90–91, 95–99, 108–9, 144–45, 146,
  153–54, 165, 167; *Beryl's Husband*,
  66–70, 78–79, 99; *Her Double Life*,
  79–80, 99
Lorin, Amii: *Morgan Wade's Woman*, 23,
  28, 29, 33, 107
Love: declaration of, 32–33; as discovery, 20; relation to sexuality,
  29–32

Marriage, 5, 8, 9, 18, 30–32, 34, 127–
  28, 145, 156, 176–77; and economic
  considerations, 128–32, 133–39;
  equality in, 140–42; and romantic
  love, 130–32, 133–39; in Victorian
  romance: 73–74, 76, 86–88, 100–102.
  See also Comic tradition
Matthaei, Julie A., 50n, 98n, 99n
Mitchell, Margaret: *Gone With the Wind*,
  4, 11–12, 145–50, 163–64, 165
Modleski, Tania, 16n, 24n, 51n, 127n,
  133, 168n, 169
Moers, Ellen, 134n

Narrative point of view, 114–15, 133

Neff, Wanda Fraiken, 96
Nelli, Rene, 129n

Other Woman, 47–49, 107, 159

Patriarchy, 5–6, 11, 57–62, 73–74, 78,
  91–92, 120, 122, 123, 131, 173, 175,
  177. *See also* Father
Peake, Lilian: *The Little Impostor*, 45, 46,
  105–6
Peters, Elizabeth (Barbara Michaels),
  15n
Phillips, David Graham: *Susan Lennox*,
  102
Poovey, Mary, 49n, 130n
Property, 3–4, 10, 11, 144, 174; in
  Austen ("Pemberley"), 133, 138–39,
  142–43; in Brontë ("Thornfield,"
  "Ferndean"), 141–42, 143; in
  Mitchell ("Twelve Oaks"), 146–47,
  149

Quest, 11, 19, 21–22, 27, 34

Radway, Janice, 6n, 9n, 15n, 17n, 19n,
  24n, 132n, 159n, 163n, 167n, 170n
Richardson, Samuel: *Clarissa*, 49;
  Pamela, 30, 49, 103, 127, 132–33,
  153, 157, 165, 174
Romance: and domesticity, 74–75;
  courtly love, 128–29; and economic
  conditions, 10–11, 57–59, 74–75,
  77–78, 90–92; as initiation, 12, 158–
  62; as idealized love relationship, 18;
  literary romance, 22; as love story, 4–
  5; as mass market genre, 3, 7–8, 18–
  19; as response to bourgeois society,
  131; and social contradictions, 157–
  58, 170–71, 176–77. *See also* Quest
Romance hero: and bourgeois society,
  57–59; as composite figure, 57–62;
  and economic power, 8–9, 41,
  49–50, 127–28, 133, 138–39, 143,
  145–50, 154; as fantasy construct,
  41, 47; as formulaic type, 42; and
  male sexuality, 23–24, 30, 155;
  as mentor, 158–64; as nurturer,

162–64; and *Playboy man*, 46–49; as psychologically wounded, 48–49, 114–16; in relation to father, 59–62; in relation to traditional hero, 53–54, 57; in relation to traditional villain, 11, 50–53, 57–58, 147-49; and sexual power, 8–9, 41, 49–50, 127–28, 133, 138–39, 143, 145–50, 154; in Victorian romance, 67–70, 76, 78, 91; and work, 42–46, 90n, 110, 116. *See also* Father; Villain

Romance hero, sources of: Austen, 4, 11, 133, 143–44; Brontë, 5, 11, 51–53, 56–57, 143–44; Mitchell, 5, 11–12, 146–50

Romance heroine: and beauty, 174–75; as career woman ("corporate heroine"), 112–22, 158, 160; as childlike, 28, 59–61, 120, 121n; as "liberated," 103, 104, 109–12, 155–56; as passive, 165–67; and self-betrayal, 168–69. *See also* Marriage; Sexuality; Work

Romance heroine, Victorian: and childhood, 79, 84–86, 91, 99–100, 159–64; and class, 82–83, 86; as genteel, 88–89; as heroic, 69, 78, 80, 82, 85–86, 87; as orphan, 82, 84, 99–100. *See also* Marriage; Sexuality; Work

Romance plot: early marriage variant, 31, 67, 106–8, 163–64; sexual plot, 18, 20–21, 22–30, 34, 36, 171; subtext, 5–6, 8, 153, 156, 176–77; surface story, 5, 8, 20–21, 153, 156, 158, 171, 176–77

Russ, Joanna, 167

Ryan, Mary P., 41n, 49n, 73n, 77, 98n, 104n, 112n, 155n, 172n

Scott, Joanna: *Corporate Policy*, 115, 117–21

Sexuality: dangers of, 25–30, 155, 156–57, 174; as expression of selfhood, 35–36; as initiation, 158–64, 169, 176–77; as internalized, 25–27, 154; and pleasure, 172; in service of love, 27–30, 155; as sign of love, 28–30, 155; as sign of womanhood, 28–29, 158–59

Shahar, Shulamith, 129n

Showalter, Elaine, 51n, 56n, 167

Simmons, Suzanne: *The Tempestuous Lovers*, 28, 31, 32, 43, 44, 109n

Snitow, Ann Barr, 17n

Social class, 98, 107

Southworth, E. D. E. N., 63, 71n

Spacks, Patricia, 56n, 166n

Stephens, Jeanne: *Wonder and Wild Desire*, 107–8

Stone, Lawrence, 8n, 130–32, 145

Surrogate father. *See* Father

Villain, 50, 56, 57–58, 61, 66–70, 76, 80, 81, 144–45, 154, 174; and relation to hero, 50–53, 57–58, 80, 84–92

Weeks, Jeffrey, 170–71, 172–73

Weibel, Kathryn, 166–67

Wentworth, Sally: *Liberated Lady*, 27, 110–12, 113, 119

White, Hayden, 6n

Whittal, Yvonne: *Season of Shadows*, 51n, 107

Wildman, Faye: *The Fletcher Legacy*, 116, 122n

Winspear, Violet: *A Girl Possessed*, 24, 26n, 45–46, 51n, 109

Work, 11, 95, 103–5; in the arts, 100, 108–9; in business, 109–22; domestic, 87, 97–98, 99–101, 105–8; vs. love, 113–21

Work (Victorian heroine): in the arts, 100; as companion, 99; as domestic, 97–98, 99–101; as governess, 87, 99

Jan Cohn is currently dean of the faculty at Trinity College in Hartford, Connecticut. A specialist in American literature and popular culture, she previously taught at George Mason University and Carnegie-Mellon University.